Words from Those Touched by Their Story

With over 62 years of marriage, Walt and Ikie offer a must-read with sage advice on maintaining a balanced and meaningful married life from both their own experiences and those passed down from their parents, all wrapped in the strong texture of biblical truth.

—Dr. Tim Walker, Minister of Music, Christ United Jackson

Life catches us off guard at times. Married couples might find themselves in doubt, afraid, and confused. Sometimes our marriage feels like it is under attack. A war is waged in our minds and the enemy uses every tool in its disposal, finances, temptation, unemployment, and friendships to weaken our relationship with our marriage partner. But the Beamon's have given us the keys to fight back. Their experiences are lessons learned to give us victory one day at a time, one battle at a time. Read the book. It will do you and your marriage good!

**—The Rev., Dr. Robert L. Jemerson,
Pastor Second Baptist Church, San Antonio, Texas**

As a nephew, I have had the privilege of watching my uncle and aunt live out the kind of marriage most only dream about-sixty plus years of love, patience, and faithfulness. As a pastor, I see in their story a living testimony of God's design for marriage, showing that commitment is not simply a promise made once, but a promise kept daily with grace. This book is more than their story; it's a guide and an inspiration for anyone who desires to build a marriage that lasts.

—Rev. Reginald Buckley, Pastor of Cade Chapel MB Church, Jackson, Mississippi

Walter and Ikie's book, *A Marriage That Endures Forever*, will help couples who are preparing to be married, been married for several years, couples experiencing troublesome times in their marriage, and those who just want to improve upon the strength of their marriage. I have been assigned as a pastor for some fifty-four years. I have had the opportunity to counsel several couples who fit the above categories. Walter and Ikie's book has garnered a wealth of knowledge during their sixty-two plus years of marriage, and they are sharing this wealth of knowledge and information with the readers. It is a great resource for ministers who have the responsibility of counselling all stages of marriage. I highly recommend this book to anyone who wants to have a dynamic marriage.

—Rev. John Paul Ruth, Presiding Elder of the Conyers-Winder District of The Georgia Conference, South Atlantic Episcopal District of the African Methodist Episcopal Zion Church

A Marriage That Endures Forever is a rare treasure of godly wisdom, totally biblical, inspired by the Spirit, and born of practical experience. Walt and Ikie Beamon are two of the most thoughtful and intellectual people I know. This book is bound to be a classic. In this book, they masterfully communicated God's plan and effective strategies of a marriage that will stand the test of time. It is a straightforward, balanced, and refreshing guide to marriage success.

—Marshall Rainge, MSgt/First Sergeant Retired USAF

Rev. Walter and Mrs. Ikie Beamon have written an excellent work for those who have been married for years, newlyweds, and those contemplating marriage. For those married with longevity, this work reminds them that the same ingredients that solidified the courtship are necessary to maintain it. Newlyweds become aware of the importance of never letting the romantic flame die as they honor their vows, while those considering marriage should ask hard questions of their perspective mates about those things that are non-negotiable in their lives. Knowing the meaning of the commitment your vows require and purposing to keep that commitment will ensure a lasting relationship.

—Rev. Merchuria Chase Williams, MDiv, Ph.D.

I have only known Walt and Ikie during their senior years, so I found this book that bridged the years from their early lives to the present to be a fascinating read. They were both transparent and authentic in what they shared, and I enjoyed hearing their personal perspectives on key events in their lives. They have been shaped by their strong foundational beliefs in their God, and their lives have shown how they trusted Him in all of the decisions they made. They made it clear that marriage isn't an easy commitment but one that is well worth the effort if you find the right partner to invest your life with. When it wasn't easy, they found ways to stay together, learn from their mistakes, and get even stronger, and there are priceless gems in this heartfelt book that will resonate with all who read it.

—Paige Stowe, Vice-President-Regulatory and Legislative Affairs for Bell South, Mississippi, Retired

When Adam professed Eve to be his wife, it became the first declaration of marriage without any formal ceremony or instructions. Their union started the godly tradition and duty of two people joining together to become one. Using their perspective parents' union installed with biblical principles as a template, Walter and Ikie's book offers their personal journey for a successful marriage. Their ingredients for success were seasoned with honoring their parents' marriage, having blind trust in each other, being effective communicators, being submissive to each other, knowing and respecting each other's boundaries, forgiving each other, being unified in parenting, and much more.

—M.K. Barnes, Retired U.S. Military Officer and Family Law Mediator

Walt and Ikie lead us on a journey to understand each of the elements that comprise the foundation of their marriage of over 62 years. From the town of Camden and a large farm in rural Jefferson Davis County in Mississippi, we learn of the strong, determined and loving marriages that they witnessed across the generations of parents, grandparents, uncles, and aunts. Walt and Ikie provide a clear refutation of the widely held misconception that lasting marriages and valuation of higher education are exceptional. They explain the key role that Tougaloo College played not only in their introduction to each other, but also in the blessing of their marriage by their parents. Walt and Ikie's book provides inspiration to couples and affirmation for families who desire and emphasize the benefits of lasting marriages. *A Marriage That Endures Forever* is ideal for Bible studies, book clubs, and those considering genealogical studies of families. Referencing the research of sociologists and specific scriptures, they explain how the examples of lasting marriages that they witnessed daily have helped sustain their trust in God and their commitment to each other.

**—Jon McCoy, MDiv, PhD, Lead Pastor,
Christ United Methodist Church, East Moline, Illinois**

A Marriage That Endures Forever is an excellent book written by the Beamon's describing their 62 years of marriage. The book gives insights into their journey of becoming one. From enduring separation during their courtship, to marriage and discovering their individual differences, they describe the essentials needed to build a strong marriage. Their writing style is from the heart and creates a personal connection with the reader. This book is Scripture-based and appropriate for any stage of marriage.

—CW5 Gordon Smith, USA, Retired

A Note from the Publisher

As the publisher of this inspiring work and someone who has personally walked the path of a long, faith-filled marriage, I offer the following words as a humble reflection on love that lasts.

"I wish my husband and I, who were married for 55 years, had the tools shared in this book during our early years together. It was tough, it was challenging, but we endured until the end. It was only by the grace of God and our commitment to wanting our marriage to last. I wish he were still here to help endorse this book, because this book truly stands as a testimony that with love, faith, patience, and perseverance, a marriage can endure forever."

—*Willa Robinson, Publisher, KP Publishing Company,*
Los Angeles, California and Las Vegas, Nevada

A Marriage

THAT ENDURES
FOREVER

OUR JOURNEY, YOUR PATH TO
A HEALTHY MARRIAGE

CHAPLAIN COLONEL, RETIRED WALTER BEAMON
& IKIE BEAMON

KP PUBLISHING COMPANY

ISBN: 979-8-994040-42-8 (Hardcover)
ISBN: 979-8-994090-43-5 (Paperback)
ISBN: 979-8-994990-44-2 (eBook)

Library of Congress Control Number: Pending

Editor: Frank A. Williams
Cover Design: Mrs. Gift Osakwe
Literary Director: Sandra Slayton James

Scripture taken from the New King James Version®. Copyright © 1982 by Thomas Nelson. Used by permission. All rights reserved.

Scripture quotations are taken from the *Holy Bible*, New Living Translation, copyright 1996, 2004, 2007, 2015 by Tyndale House Foundation. Used by permission of Tyndale House Publishers, Inc., Carol Stream, Illinois 60188. All rights reserved.

Scripture quotations are from the *ESV® Bible (The Holy Bible, English Standard Version®)*, Copyright © 2001 by Crossway, a publishing ministry of Good News Publishers. Used by permission. All rights reserved.

Scripture taken from THE HOLY BIBLE, NEW INTERNATIONAL VERSION®. Copyright © 1973, 1978, 1984, 2011 by Biblica, Inc.™. Used by permission of Zondervan

Scripture taken from the *Complete Jewish Bible*. Copyright © 1998 by David H. Stern. Published by Jewish New Testament Publications, Inc. Used by permission. All rights reserved.

Published by:

KP Publishing Company
Publisher of Fiction, Nonfiction & Children's Books
Las Vegas, NV 89117
www.kp-pub.com

Printed in the United States of America

Dedication

This book is dedicated to our deceased parents, Clement and Earnestine Beamon and Isaac and Lillie Mae Haynes. We learned from their demonstration of life values some of the requirements necessary for a healthy, successful marriage.

Contents

Foreword

I have been acquainted with the authors, Walter, and Ikie Beamon, for over fifty years. Our relationship began in 1970 when Walter was appointed pastor of Shaw Temple A.M.E. Zion Church in Atlanta, Georgia. They had been married for only seven years. During this time, Ikie and I became close friends, and a few years later, I was humbled when they asked me to be the godmother of their infant son, Tony.

The assignment to Shaw Temple presented challenges in the Beamon's marital and ministerial journey. Walt had limited pastoral experience, and this was his third church appointment, including two small churches while a seminary student. They had moved to a large city to lead a church that was facing "major issues." With much prayer and commitment, they overcame the obstacles and had a memorable and successful five-year pastoral ministry. The church membership grew rapidly under his leadership and became a prominent congregation in the denomination.

Since they left Shaw, we have maintained a close relationship for more than 50 years. During a recent visit with Walt and Ikie, they shared their intention to write a book on marriage. Having witnessed their journey and heard many of their stories, my response was, Why not? Anyone who can stay together for sixty-two years must have a wealth of knowledge and experience to share that will help others to build and sustain a healthy marriage.

I have observed their genuine love, unwavering commitment, and resilience in navigating challenges, which has emerged into a strong and lasting relationship. I recall attending and participating in their 50th wedding anniversary celebration and how they interacted with each other with so much love and admiration. You would have thought it was their initial wedding day.

This book, *A Marriage That Endures Forever*, is for you whether you are happy or experiencing problems in your marriage; whether you have been married for one year, sixty years, or are anticipating marriage. The Beamon's share with the reader a detailed chronology of their sixty-two-year marital journey. You will find that they are very open and honest about the "good, bad, and ugly." They make it clear that, for them, marriage was not always wine and roses. However, they are committed to the vows they made to each other in 1963; to have and to hold from this day forward, for better or for worse, for richer or poorer, in sickness and in health, until death us do part.

Being devout Christians, they have found their strong faith and belief in the sanctity of marriage to be their foundation for staying the course during challenging times. Additionally, much of what they learned about building and sustaining a successful marriage came from observing their wonderful parents. You will read firsthand accounts of their parents' relationships and how they helped shape their lasting marriage.

You might ask, "Why do we need another book on marriage? What is different about this one?" I would venture to say that there aren't many "self-help" books on this subject written by couples who have been married for more than six decades. Of note, the Beamons are from the Silent Generation (born between 1928 and 1945). You might further ask, "Why is this important?" Many of the characteristics of this generation are essential in building and sustaining a successful marriage. They are loyal to their religious beliefs, relationships, and their families. They value teamwork, cooperation, and stability. They exhibit strength and a strong sense of determination in difficult and challenging times. While reading, you will see evidence of these traits in the Beamons throughout the book.

The sixty-two-year marriage of Walt and Ikie shows the strength of two people committed to building a life together. Their journey shares experiences that are inspiring and enlightening. They demonstrate that a lasting partnership and true love are built through dedication, honest communication, mutual respect, trust, and steadfast support.

A Marriage That Endures Forever is a collection of spiritual and practical advice that shows that a lasting, fulfilling marriage is possible for all couples. I commend my friends for the sacrifices they made in writing this book, so that others may enjoy committed love and a long-lasting marriage, as they have had for 62 years.

Dorothy Williams & son, Tony

—Dorothy W. Williams, Director of Pharmacy
Emory University Hospital Midtown (Ret)

Introduction

Statistics from 2023 show that the institution of marriage is in serious trouble. According to the American Psychological Association, 40-50 percent of marriages in the United States end in divorce. The Centers for Disease Control (CDC) and Prevention's National Center for Health Statistics (NCHS) published data showing rate trends from statistics that showed the trend of divorce rates from 1900 to 2021. These figures reveal that American divorce rates climbed steadily over the last 150 years, only beginning to decline in the 1990s.

Numerous factors contribute to the rise and fall of divorce rates. However, a lack of commitment is most commonly cited as the leading cause of divorce. Many couples also list infidelity, unrealistic expectations, and ongoing conflict as major contributing factors. While these statistics serve as a general benchmark, it's important to understand that divorce rates can vary depending on factors such as age, education, and socio-economic status.

More recent statistics indicate that the divorce rate has declined over the last 20 years. Several theories have been proposed to explain this trend. First, people are delaying marriage until they are older. Individuals who wait until after age 25 are 24 percent less likely to get a divorce. Second, there is an increase in social permissiveness, with more people choosing to cohabit rather than marry. Third, many young adults are returning home to live with their parents rather than pursuing marriage early in life.

For some, marriage represents a deep commitment, and that commitment can feel overwhelming. This fear is classified as gamophobia—an irrational fear of long-term partnership or marriage. People who have gamophobia may view marriage like a bar of soap: It looks and smells good until you bite into it.

So, why did Ikie and I choose to write a book on marriage? It's worth noting that we have been in a healthy marriage for more than 62 years. Ikie has not authored a book, and I had not considered writing another after completing my memoir, *Inmates in Charge*.

However, in February of 2024, Willa Robinson, the publisher of that book, suggested we should seriously consider writing one together. Willa had traveled to The Two Museums in Jackson, Mississippi, for the first book signing of my recently published work. During one of our conversations, she discovered how long we had been married and strongly encouraged us to co-author a book on marriage. She believed we had valuable insights to share that could benefit others. After she left, Ikie and I had several very long, heartfelt discussions and eventually agreed to take on the task.

It is our desire and prayer that married couples, whether they are facing challenges or not, as well as those preparing for marriage, will find our beliefs and experiences helpful. The insights shared in this book are based on biblical principles, our personal experiences and challenges, the examples set by our parents' marriages, and the marriages of others we've observed.

There are many perspectives on the subject of marriage. The one by Simone Signoret, a French actress speaks to us very clearly and forcefully. She said, *"Chains do not hold a marriage together. It is threads, hundreds of tiny threads, which sew people together through the years."*

Not all of our beliefs will apply to every relationship. Since there are no perfect people, there are no perfect marriages. As such, we do not claim that this book will solve every marital issue. We've also chosen to avoid using real names when referring to other people. Throughout the book, we have presented our thoughts or ***beliefs*** on specific issues as **bold, italicized statements to distinguish them clearly.**

We do not consider ourselves marriage experts. We are not licensed counselors or authorities on the subject. However, we have been deeply blessed to have the patience, resilience, and willingness to put in the hard work necessary to make our marriage thrive—despite our differences and the challenges we have faced.

As mentioned earlier, our beliefs are rooted in Scripture. Ikie and I are Christians, and as you read this book, you'll see how our actions in various situations reflected our understanding of biblical teachings. This understanding strengthened our pursuits of the biblical principle of *oneness* between husband and wife.

This is our story. Through the providence of God, we found each other, and the rest is history.

Chapter 1

IMPACT OF ROLE MODELING ON OUR MARRIAGE

"Listen my son, to your father's instruction and do not forsake your mother's teaching. They are a garland to grace your head and a chain to adorn your neck."

Proverbs 1:8-9 (NIV)

WALT & IKIE

Our marriage has been successful and happy for more than 62 years, in part, because of the role modeling of our parents in their marriages. As we grew up, we observed happiness and longevity in their marriages. Both of us were blessed to witness and observe the interactions in their marriages for more than 60 years.

For this reason, we will share information about our parents in this chapter. We will reference their marriages several times in succeeding chapters of the book.

Appropriate role modeling in marriages is valuable during the formative years of children.

It's important to note that we understand many children are not exposed to this kind of role modeling in marriage. Many children today are growing up in "broken homes." According to Dr. Patrick Capriola, MD Psychiatry, "a broken home is a household that is no longer functioning as a family unit." Broken homes can be caused by addiction, death, poverty, violence, marital problems, poor family relationships, and other factors. Families don't have to be separated in order to be in a broken home. A broken home is a description of **family dysfunction**.

Many adults who are anticipating marriage or who are already married may not have experienced the role modeling that we did. Others are in the home together, miserably trying to maintain a dysfunctional family unit. We share the stories of our parents with you for two reasons. First, their stories may provide something that is inspirational or beneficial to someone. And secondly, as our stories are shared, we will often refer to fundamental beliefs that were learned from the role modeling of our parents. We are going to provide information about our parents and their role modeling.

WALT

Walt's parents

My parents, Clement and Earnestine Beamon, grew up in the back woods of Camden, Mississippi. My dad was born in 1906 and my mother in 1918. Dad was the youngest son of 10 children and inherited his family's small two-bedroom wooden, framed house, which I described in detail in my memoir, *Inmates in Charge*. I have a vivid memory of the rustic surroundings of my early home. During this time, life was very simple. My family did not have television until I was in my early teens, and our only radio was battery operated. In other words, there were very few things that interrupted the routines of our day-to-day life.

The lack of interruptions provided "quality" family time. Quality family time for me included having plenty of time to interact with my parents and siblings, listening to the wisdom in discussions between my

7

parents and grandparents, attending our small Methodist church, and the list goes on.

This formative period of my life was pivotal in developing character traits that I have carried into my adult years and into our marriage.

Quality time should be spent with children in their formative years, and is valuable in the development of their core values.

King Solomon in, Proverbs 5:1 (NIV) gave great counsel to his son, saying, **"My son pay attention to my wisdom; listen carefully to my wise counsel."** Family time spent sharing meals and experiences together, communicating, establishing boundaries, and establishing family traditions will be beneficial throughout an individual's life.

Dad was an elementary school teacher; my mother was a stay-at-home spouse. I am the oldest surviving son with four younger sisters, Myra, Agnes, Vivian, and Elaine. As the oldest and only living son, my parents expected me to complete all of my assigned tasks thoroughly and entirely.

Children should know what is expected of them at an early age. They should also know the consequences of not meeting those expectations.

At the age of 9-10 years, I was expected to herd the family's 6 to 8 milk cows every evening and milk them every morning. Feeding the hogs daily was on my list of duties. I was also expected to gather wood and kindling for our cookstove and fireplace. There were no natural gas pipelines or electricity available in our neck of the woods at the time. I did not have to wonder what my responsibilities were. These chores and others helped me to develop a work ethic that became ingrained and automatic in my daily activities. These high expectations helped to prepare me for greater responsibilities in my adult life as a father and husband.

In my early years of elementary and junior high school, there were no public schools in our area. Most children attended school in a local Black church, Murphy Chapel African Methodist Episcopal Zion Church (AME Zion), located in the little quaint town of Camden. We had no bus transportation until I was a junior high student around 1953. In fact, not only was my dad the principal of our (two teacher) elementary school during those early years, but to subsidize his meager salary as a school-teacher later, he drove a school bus for extra pay when the school attendance grew much larger.

His starting salary as a schoolteacher was about $50.00 a month. When he took on the responsibility of driving the bus his salary increased gradually. The combination of his teaching salary and bus driving roughly totaled $250 a month. This was during the 50s. However, you must understand that $250.00 per month for Black school teachers in rural communities, in the Jim Crow South, was pretty good money when compared with other Blacks in the community. Dad used every opportunity to increase his income to enhance our quality of life.

As I matured and became a husband and father, I remembered Dad's work ethic in providing for the needs of our family.

I am still amazed when I reflect on how my dad provided for our family on such a small income. This became instructive to me when I became of age and became the "man of the house" in our marriage.

Children should see their parents actively working to effectively provide for their family.

I recall statements that Dad made that have impacted me to this day. **"If you don't accomplish more than I did, you would have failed! You have far more and better opportunities than I ever had. So, do your best. Don't be lazy! Don't take shortcuts. Do it right the first time!"** All those verbal comments, instructions, and advice that Dad gave—I internalized. Now, looking back over the years, I realize that I have tried to emulate those things in my life, specifically as a husband and father. His words of wisdom became my encouragement, and they became important to me when I left home, became a man and entered into holy matrimony.

I have mentioned that Dad was a great provider for our family. He financially provided for us by taking advantage of various opportunities to increase his income. Dad was also the primary "grocery shopper." He took pride in buying large quantities of food. There were five of us children, so he bought lots of food, especially fruits. Although we were not rich, I can truthfully say we never knew hunger and enjoyed many foods that most children living in our neighborhood could not afford.

Unfortunately, I have emulated this behavior or practice by buying too much food ever since Ikie and I got married. I tend to shop for groceries and always buy too much food. This practice hasn't gone well in our household because Ikie prefers to do the grocery shopping. She frequently reminds me that there are only two of us here now, and before our kids grew up and left home, she would remind me that we only had two children, not five.

This issue was not a problem for my mother because she did not mind that Dad did the grocery shopping. She was content sending a grocery list of needed food. In fact, Mama did not enjoy grocery shopping. But this issue has always been problematic for Ikie. Her position was, "I know better than you about what we need, and I hate wasting food."

Most marriages have some perpetual differences that may never be resolved.

We have not resolved this issue yet, but we have made compromises. Ikie makes a list of our definite household needs and she shops for those. She has accepted the fact that I am going to shop for something at the grocery store. To appease me, she sometimes give me a list of things to buy, especially if we are hosting dinner. She knows I enjoy going to the store even though I may duplicate something she already has or buy too much. By following this practice we are both somewhat pleased and satisfied.

> *"It's better to live in the corner of an attic than with a quarrelsome wife (husband) in a lovely home."*
>
> Proverbs 21:9 (NIV)

Let me share a bit about my mother. My mother was 12 years younger than my dad. Some might say that—"**my dad robbed the cradle!**" They had to elope to get married. My grandparents would not approve of their marriage because they felt that Mama was too young to marry a man twelve years her senior. Dad and Mama attended the same church, and their families knew each other very well.

My mother's dad was a farmer and her mother a housewife. Mama, as I was told, was a very attractive woman, especially during her youth. I have also been told that Dad made the statement, "**One day**, **I'm going to marry that pretty girl!**" Some years later, when she was old enough and they were ready, he contacted a minister who was a friend and persuaded him to perform the ceremony in his home and to keep their marriage secret. Dad had watched Mama grow from infancy into a young woman. Apparently, he had fallen in love with her long before they were married. Undoubtedly, he believed that she would be the one to bring joy and happiness into his life.

I saw Mama and Dad as stable, committed partners who were devoted to each other. I saw two people who enjoyed each other's company. As youngsters, growing up, we would often hear Dad and Mama laughing and talking with each other while sitting on the porch or riding in the car and often long after retiring for the evening.

Children who live in homes with family experiences of security, love, stimulation, and positive interactions will usually have successful marriages.

I never recall hearing our parents being verbally abusive to each other. There was no name-calling or disrespect directed at each other. Even at that early age, I naturally wanted a future marriage similar to theirs.

Dad loved and provided for his family economically, emotionally, and spiritually, and ensured that we were protected from many of society's ills. He was an educator and disciplinarian. Mama was a sweet spirited, wonderful homemaker and a very kindhearted person. Whenever we really wanted something that required our parents' approval, Mama was the one we approached first, most of the time.

Mama did not finish high school as she had hoped. During the 1920s, 30s, and 40s there were no public high schools available for Blacks in her area. However, she was determined to finish high school. She met the requirements necessary to get a GED after the age of 50. Mama worked outside the home after acquiring the GED as an assistant HeadStart teacher for about ten years.

Over the years, I have reflected on the character traits of both of my parents. I tend to think more about my mother's marital behaviors, being loyal to my dad and nurturing my siblings and me. When Ikie and I became serious in our relationship, I realized that she possessed some of the qualities of my mother that I admired. I have often heard that girls generally marry men with traits similar to their fathers and men marry women with traits similar to their mothers. I was curious as to whether or not this was true. According to Joseph Nicolosi, an American clinical psychologist, in an article called *Myth or Fact —We Marry a Version of our Mother or Father,* research has shown that:

We are not only biologically predisposed to certain physical illnesses, strengths, and weaknesses but also psychologically. We subconsciously absorb our parents' habits, behaviors, mannerisms, and attitudes, and mirror them.

The home my father inherited from his parents was located about two miles from the main highway. The road, which may be more accurately called a lane, was clay dirt and very narrow without any gravel. Mama always wanted to move from the old home place. She really wanted to move to an urban area, like Canton, which was 13 miles away.

But she and Dad **compromised**, and Dad built a small wooden framed house without a bathroom, about a fourth of a mile from the main highway in 1956. It was built on the acreage we owned. Mama was happy because we were now close enough to see the highway traffic from our home. She was able to see vehicles, some of whom she knew, travelling back and forth and felt liberated and happy. The mail carrier brought our mail within fifty yards of our house, whereas before we moved, our mailbox along with neighbors were together on the main highway, two miles from our old house.

Years later, in 1970, Dad built their retirement home, a beautiful, modern 3-bedroom, brick, ranch style home which brought much joy to her life! All my siblings and their families looked forward to coming back home and our parents were so very happy to have us gather there on many occasions. We had lots of fun and enjoyed being together. It was akin to having a family reunion. I witnessed many compromises in their marriage. This stuck with me, and I carried that virtue into my marriage.

It is important for children to see their parents resolve differences of opinions through understanding and compromise.

During my formative years, our parents set standards of faith values. Dad as the head of our household set the tone. He was a godly man, who loved his family and wanted all of us to be saved, or come to know Jesus Christ in the pardon of our sins. When it came to church attendance, he, and Mama made sure we were there. Ikie and I believe that children should grow up knowing the parent's faith standards at an early age. Parents should show examples for the children to emulate, not just speak it. There was never a question as to whether or not we were going to church, they did not send us to church while they remained at home. Dad was a leader in our little church. He served as Sunday School Superintendent for more than forty years. He was also a trustee for many years.

Because they agreed in their desire to serve God together, they demonstrated a path for us. Mama was also very active in the church. She sang in the choir and loved it. As a result of her love for music, all my siblings and I sang in our little choir. She loved home mission work and loved to prepare food and take to the sick and less fortunate in the community. Their faith values, love **for** each other kept them together until their deaths. They were happily married for over 60 years.

Now you might question whether my parents were ever angry with each other, or disagreed with one another. The answer is a resounding, YES! Of course they did. However, they found a way to communicate effectively without harboring anger. They affirmed the Apostle Paul's admonition to the church at Ephesus when he stated,

> *"Be angry, but don't sin. Don't let the sun go down before you have dealt with the cause of your anger."*
>
> Ephesians. 4:26 (CJB)

Parents' role modeling of their faith impacts the children's faith.
My parents took their marital vows to each other very seriously. They knew and affirmed the scriptures such as Genesis 2:24 (NIV) which states that:

> **"a man should leave his father and mother and be united to his wife."**

They treasured 1 Corinthians 13, which describes love as **patient, kind, selfless, hopes all things, endures all things, bears all things. Love never ends!** They took to heart the mandate from the Apostle Paul.

IKIE

I have never heard how or where my parents met. There were three girls in my family, and no brothers. Selma, who was six years older than me, and Barbara (Barb), who was three years older than me. Both are deceased. According to Selma, who was the most knowledgeable about our family history, our parents eloped.

Ikie's parents and family

Ikie's Father with grandson

My parents' family backgrounds could not have been more different. Both of my parents were born in May of 1906. Daddy was six days older than mama. They were both raised in Jefferson Davis County of Mississippi but in different areas of the county. Because of Selma's knowledge, I always knew that our parent's family dynamics, socio-economic and educational status were very different.

The most prominent factors they seemed to have in common were the size of their families and the fact that they grew up on farms. Daddy grew up on a small farm. Mama also grew up on a farm, but it was much larger. They were both born into large families.

Daddy had eight siblings that I knew well. They lived near where I grew up. At one time, at least four of his siblings lived within one half mile of each other. Most of my aunts and uncles were married to the same spouses until one of them died. Longevity in marriage was natural to me because I observed this not only with parents but also with my aunts and uncles. Long successful marriages were what I knew and was what I expected in my own marriage.

My fraternal grandparents, aunts and uncles were not educated or trained in any particular skills. My uncles were poor farmers who owned a few acres of land used to farm vegetables, cotton and grow timber. My aunts were typical farmer's wives who canned vegetables, preserved pork and beef from animals that were slaughtered on their farms. Preservation of food was a way of life for our family. Foods preserved by canning or freezing was how we all got through the year. I observed these behaviors of my aunts and my mother all my young life. It was so instilled into me that I won a state award in Food Preservation through the Four-H Club. To this day, as we write this book, I still preserve food in our freezers from our garden. My mother always cooked more than enough for a meal to have leftovers. We ate leftovers and we wanted enough in case somebody came by and needed or wanted a meal. I still purposefully cook more than enough in order to freeze some foods. I do this so I can have most of the meals already cooked and simply add to them. Doing this, I avoid having to cook entire meals.

Children learn and grow from observing habits of adults and these habits become lifetime behaviors.

I did not know either of my fraternal grandparents. My fraternal grandfather died when Daddy was a young boy. I am told that he owned a small amount of land when he died, but the young family was left very poor and needy. When Grandpa passed, Daddy and his older brother, Uncle Allen (nick-named Dub), had to drop out of elementary school to help Grandma raise food in vegetable gardens as well as cotton and corn. They also took on any odd jobs they could find to earn money to help support their family. Daddy was in the fifth grade when he had to drop out of school. He was never able to go back to school, but he had more "mother wit" than most people with education and/or training.

At some point before he and Mama married, Daddy owned a small amount of land. He worked hard on the farm and, on railroads, building tracks. Eventually, with income from cotton, the sale of vegetables from truck crops, and the income from Mama's teaching position, we owned more than 100 acres of land.

The first house that I remember, as a child, had three small bedrooms, a kitchen and what we call a dining room. That room had a table and some chairs, a bench (where we girls ate) and an ice box. Around that table, I learned my first Bible verse at about three years of age, "Jesus wept." Each of us had to repeat a Bible verse after Daddy gave "grace" before we ate. It was at that table that I heard my parents pray. While sitting at that table or sitting on the porch, I learned family rules like listening, obeying, and the importance of honesty.

Years later, when I was about ten years old, my parents built another larger home which Daddy always referred to as his "big house." The new house had four bedrooms, a living room, a dining room, a kitchen, and eventually an indoor bathroom!

My parents functioned together like a well-oiled machine. In fact, my earliest understanding of teamwork resulted from their examples. As I mentioned, Mama was an elementary school teacher. However, she never learned to drive. Consequently, Daddy had to drive her everywhere she needed to go. He started teaching me how to drive by the time I was about thirteen. Until I was old enough to drive, they were together most of the time. People would often say, "When you see Ike (Daddy's nickname), you will see Lillie Mae (Mama)." For Mama to teach, my daddy would have to delay starting his work on our farm to drive her to school. When it was time for her to come home, he would stop work and go pick her up. That's just how it was. There was no bickering about it. It was just what had to be done. When I was old enough to get a permit and a driver's license, I was able to help with the task of driving Mama where she needed to go.

During cotton picking season, Daddy would hire field hands to help us pick cotton. Although Daddy could figure out what their pay should be, Mama would automatically write everything down on paper. So as Daddy weighed the cotton, Mama kept up with each person's number of pounds of cotton and helped Daddy pay the correct amount of money due the worker. In the summer months when Mama was not teaching, she worked in the field with the rest of us. But around 10:30 am she would go to the house to cook dinner. In those days, dinner was eaten at midday rather than later in the day.

The concept of working as a team enhances and solidifies marriages.

Each partner should have a desire to work with their partner to accomplish a desired goal. Over our many years of marriage Walt and I have worked as a team. We would discuss our desired goals and decide on what we feel is the best approach to reach them. Sometimes I had special assignments and sometimes he had some, but we worked at the projects together. That has definitely enhanced our marriage.

Mama was not only a teacher at school but at home as well. When she, my sisters and I were gathering, preparing, and preserving vegetables from our farm or berries and plums from the woods, she would always teach us something. One of her most frequent talks was about "how to be a lady." Those talks about being a lady were so frequent that I sometimes would have preferred getting a spanking than hearing them again. Included in these instructions were subjects on how to sit, how to walk, what to say, table-setting, proper tone, and conversation for a woman, and more.

Mama had attended Tougaloo College and had grown up in an atypical African American Mississippi home. She had done a lot of reading so she was knowledgeable in these areas. Some other areas I learned from Mama were sewing, knitting, and crocheting. I have used these skills in some way during our entire marriage. Now, as I age, I still sew sometime. I am reminded of the scripture,

> *"Train a child in the way he should go; even when he is old, he will not depart from it."*
>
> Proverbs 22:6 (NIV)

Mama was a stickler for cleanliness. We had to leave our house clean every time we went somewhere. She taught us to leave our home clean enough for the president to visit at any time, unannounced. I have attempted to carry these qualities into our marriage. When our children were growing up, I was constantly "picking up" after them. When we first got married, I made the mistake of complaining to Mother Earnestine that I was having to pick up after Walt. Her response, *"He never had to pick up before, but if you get tired of him being messy, send him back home!"*

I assumed she was joking, but, needless to say, I never complained to her again about his messes. Despite my efforts, Walt will never be as clean as me.

I learned early in my life how to "stretch" a dollar. We will talk more about this in a later chapter. Both of my parents were very thrifty with spending. Part of my father's early years were during the "Great Depression" when resources and food were scarce. In those days he did not have enough food. As a result of those very lean years, even in his adult years, he always felt there was a definite need to hunt, fish or do whatever he could to put food on the table for his family. By any economic standard, from his childhood to his early adult life, he would have been considered "poor."

I feel that the uncertainties of his childhood affected how he thought about spending money. **He never believed in any kind of debt**! If he bought anything, usually he would have saved up enough money to purchase it with cash. If he had a debt at all it was during planting season for fertilizer and seeds. He would pay that off as soon as he had enough cash from the sale of cotton or truck crops such as beans, peppers, cucumbers, etc. This way of managing money became a challenge for us in our marriage because I adopted their way of managing money and Walt thought differently.

Mama also had eight siblings. She was born into a more prestigious family. Mama's family would not have been considered "poor" for an African American family living in the state of Mississippi. Two of my uncles spent some time in the military. One of them became a successful carpenter. Another uncle migrated "up north" and became a lawyer. Mama and one of her sisters were teachers. In those days, Black women who had a high school diploma could teach in rural elementary schools as long as they continued pursuing their college degree. Grandpa George and Grandma Leana, my mother's parents, had a very large home with many acres of land. As a young girl, I loved visiting my maternal grand-parents' home. They had a huge house with a large yard filled with all kinds of blooming flowers.

As I mentioned, considering the distance from each other in the county we don't know how my parents met. Daddy was an uneducated, unchurched farmer who had the reputation of being a "rabble rouser" and my mother was an educated, prim, and proper church-going, school-teacher. From what I have been told after marrying Mama, Daddy became a different man. We do know that they felt it was necessary to elope with no family members present in the parlor of some minister when they were both at age 29. We find it interesting that both sets of our parents found it necessary to elope, though for different reasons.

I was told that my parents probably eloped for several reasons. First and foremost, my grandparents did not feel that Daddy or his family were good enough for Mama. A second reason was that Mama, one of the older children, was helping her family financially with her teaching income.

My grandparents did not want to lose that income. I learned, after I became an adult, that my grandparents had cut Mama off (had no dealings with her) for months after she married Daddy.

Couples who are mature enough to recognize their devotion to each other should make up their own minds about marriage, even if they do not have the blessings of their parents.

That decision may cause bad feelings between the parents and the adult child. Mama and Daddy, at age 29, were old enough to make the decision to marry without the consent of her parents. In most families, after time and effort, the relationship between parent and adult child can be restored as it was with my parents and grandparents when Selma was born.

I cannot imagine the stress and anxiety that Mama must have felt when she made a conscious decision to defy her parents' wishes by marrying my dad, knowing he did not meet their approval.

Decisions made in life and marriage will change lives for the better or worse.

Mama's faith in God and His guidance changed the course of her life. My parents understood each other and accepted each other's differences—which were huge. They recognized that the weakness of one partner provided an opportunity for the other partner to be strong. I have never heard either of my parents speak poorly of my grandparents.

Faith, commitment, communication, transparency, and trust can sustain a marriage during the most challenging times.

This knowledge about my parents has definitely had a great influence on my behaviors and beliefs during our marriage. You will see evidence of how the actions of a strong faith in God, commitment to each other, transparency in our behaviors, and trust in each other sustained us when we faced challenges and were forced to make difficult decisions. We have often reflected on Mama's decision to marry Daddy despite of her parents. Her demonstration of love, commitment, and sacrifice was inspirational for both of us.

Psalms 32:8 (NIV) says, *"I will instruct and teach you in the way you should go; I will counsel you with my loving eye on you."*

Mama knew that God promised to guide her and offer His counsel, showing her the way with His divine wisdom. God desires the best for us in our lives and in our marriages. Couples who believe this, should remember that God's guidance may not be immediate. We must prayerfully request it and wait patiently for it.

REFLECTION AND DISCUSSION QUESTIONS

1. How have your parents' or caregivers' marriages influenced your understanding of what marriage should look like?

2. What positive examples from your upbringing would you like to carry into your own relationship?

3. Were there any negative patterns you witnessed that you want to break in your marriage?

4. How can couples intentionally serve as positive role models for their children or others?

5. In what ways can faith or values help strengthen your marriage when challenges arrive?

Chapter 2

GOD BROUGHT US TOGETHER

*"For I know the plans I have for you, declares the Lord,
plans for welfare and not for evil, to give you a future and
a hope."*

Jeremiah 29:11 (ESV)

WALT AND IKIE

Do you believe in coincidences or luck when it comes to life and circumstances? Looking back over our lives, we are compelled to answer this question by emphatically saying, "absolutely not."

God intervenes in our lives even when we don't realize it, for our good.

If we had been asked this question in 1960, when we were much younger, we would have said that our meeting was simply "luck." In other words, just being at the right place at the right time. At that time, we lacked maturity and spiritual knowledge about life and how God works. Now, we realize luck has no place now or then in our lives. With maturity we realized that luck is not a part of who God is and what He does. There are no coincidences or accidents with God.

Even though we were not praying for the opportunity to meet our future spouses, God knew who they should and would be. If you are seeking your life partner, we recommend that you pray for the right person to cross your path. We did not pray for this, but our parents probably did. It doesn't hurt to have others praying on your behalf.

WALT

Ikie and I met during my senior year at Tougaloo Southern Christian College (Tougaloo College), located in Jackson, Mississippi, in October of 1960. In fact, I had gone to a Halloween dance in the gymnasium on campus. It was a beautiful autumn evening. It wasn't too hot or too cool. As I recall, more than sixty years ago, the climate was just right for one searching for a girlfriend. I was a senior and had not found anyone with whom I felt comfortable in having a serious relationship. There were perhaps 150 to 200 students there listening and dancing to the popular music of the day. Rock and Roll music was being played by a local disc jockey (DJ). My roving eyes spotted a beautiful young ebony female, whom I had only seen on campus a few times since the new school year had begun. I'm not sure that I knew her name, but that gave me the incentive to formally meet her—Ikie Haynes.

I was a bit shy, an introvert, but with my heart pounding I just had to get to know this lovely, vivacious young lady. When the DJ played slow-paced music, my time had come, so I rushed to get ahead of any other guys to ask her for a dance. I must confess that I wasn't much of a dancer, however, I was going to dance that night. She graciously accepted my invitation to dance and that was heavenly.

When one meets the right person, there usually is a certain chemistry that feels "right."

I suggest that individuals should trust their instincts. If I had not felt comfortable with Ikie or if she had not accepted my advances, our lives would probably have been different, and this book would not be written. As we became acquainted with each other through small talk and sharing information about our backgrounds, we discovered that we shared some crucial commonalities. Those things we had in common became the foundation on which we built our relationship.

Individuals seeking relationships should look for areas of commonalities. The common areas of experiences, goals or interests will enhance the possibility of a lasting, wholesome relationship.

When the DJ played fast rhythmic music, I couldn't dance without embarrassing myself and Ikie. She was a good dancer, and fast music didn't bother her. But it was awkward for me, I had two left feet. Every time a slow song was played, I made my way to her, and we danced cheek-to-cheek. There was one young fella who was a gifted singer. He had a voice that was a good replica of the well-known pop artist, Brook Benton of the 1950s. He also had an interest in Ikie. I wanted to make sure that she spent the last moments that evening with me. Toward the end of the evening, while we danced to slow music. I asked her if I could escort her back to her dormitory. She agreed and that began our wonderful courtship.

Robert Fulghum, author of the book titled *True Love,* says**. "We're all a little weird. And life is a little weird. And when we find someone, whose weirdness is compatible with ours, we join up with them and fall into mutually satisfying weirdness-and call it love-true love."**

IKIE

I had established several very specific goals that I felt were necessary to move toward a career in the medical field. When I first came to Tougaloo, I was sure it would be to become a Registered Nurse. After getting there and interacting with other biology majors who were pursuing other areas of medicine, I became torn between a career as a nurse or doctor. After Walt and I met I started to have second thoughts about medicine. When it became obvious to me that we were sincerely interested in each other, I decided definitely on nursing since medicine would take longer to complete.

I wanted to be very successful at Tougaloo for several reasons. Firstly, I wanted to compete with my two older sisters who had been honor students throughout their four years at Alcorn College. Secondly, I always desired to make my parents proud of me. Thirdly, I love learning and research, so I wanted to learn as much as I could. To achieve these goals, I had decided to spend at least 85% of my time in the library and in the biology and chemistry labs preparing to write papers, take tests or perform experiments.

The evening we met at the dance, I had actually planned to go to the library instead of going to the dance. My three roommates were attending the social in the gym, and they convinced me to go as well. I was not interested in socializing; I thought it would be a waste of time. But I had lived off campus my first year and had not met many other students. This dance was sort of a "get to know your schoolmates" event. I decided to go. My intention was to just observe and meet a few people.

The gymnasium was crowded when my roommates and I arrived. They started dancing right away. I spotted some chairs that had been placed around the walls of the gym. I took a seat in one and started observing the people dancing and having fun. There were a few times that I observed Walt looking my way, but I looked away. Finally, he made his way over next to me and said something like, "Hi I'm Walter Beamon, who might you be?" That was a real he-man approach I suppose, and I laughed inwardly for such a corny statement. I smiled and said, "I'm Ikie Haynes." He had a deep, rich voice and intense eyes. He had a warm smile and seemed calm and relaxed.

We started talking about where we were from, what year of college we were in, and what our majors were. I was amazed when I found out he was a biology major also. I found myself having fun when he asked me for a dance and on slow and mellow music, we danced the night away. I was a good dancer, not great, but good. I will not say our meeting was "love at first sight," there was something about him that I found refreshing and "right." We danced to all the slow music and in between we got more acquainted.

Our conversation, above the loud music, was transparent, not flashy, not grandiose, or pretentious. Neither of us monopolized the conversation talking only about ourselves. Instead, we would ask each other questions. There didn't seem to be anything we were trying to hide from each other.

I was honest and truthful with my responses. And I felt he was giving me honest and truthful facts about himself.

Politeness and truthfulness in the initial meeting are crucial factors for building a strong friendship and lasting relationship.

We were very comfortable talking with each other. From our conversations, I discovered several areas of commonality. We had both grown up in rural communities on farms. My father was a farmer and my mother an educator and his father was an educator and mother a housewife. I had two sisters, and he had four. I was a biology major and so was he. I would be leaving Tougaloo for nursing school at the end of the school year while he would be graduating at the end of the school year and begin his new career of teaching.

Individuals should connect with others by being themselves honest and truthful, from the very beginning.

If one finds that it is necessary to pretend to be who they are not, the relationship will usually get off on the "wrong foot" from the beginning. The real **"YOU"** will eventually emerge, and unnecessary "bad feelings" could result, and the potential relationship is already doomed to failure. A lasting relationship should be based on truth, not pretension. Honesty in relationships promotes love and longevity. Most people will agree that they look for honesty in their partner. In fact, the lack of honesty is just a way of lying, and no relationship will develop or last with lies. Honesty is never one's enemy. Honesty is the first step towards establishing compatibility and love.

REFLECTION AND DISCUSSION QUESTIONS

1. Do you believe in coincidences or Divine intervention when it comes to relationships? Why or why not?

2. What role has prayer (yours or others') played in your relationship journey?

3. What commonalities do you share with your spouse or partner that strengthens your bond?

4. Why is honesty and truthfulness especially important in the early stages of a relationship?

Chapter 3

OUR COURTSHIP BEGINS

"Do two walk together, unless they have agreed to meet?"

Amos 3:3 (ESV)

WALT

That evening as I walked with Ikie back to her dormitory, I don't think my feet ever touched the ground. I had been a student at Tougaloo for three years and had met several young women, but never had I felt the way I did after meeting her. The chemistry between us felt genuine and natural—like something that had been waiting to happen.

When I got to my dorm, my roommates noticed right away that something had changed. One of them laughed and said, "**Man you've been bitten really good**." They were right. I couldn't wipe the grin off my facie if I tried.

Couples should have some commonalities or some areas of agreement in their backgrounds, personalities, behaviors, or goals to have a foundation on which to build the relationship they desire.

IKIE

As I walked with him toward my dorm, I realized I was smiling to myself. There was something special about him, something steady and sincere. I didn't know it yet, but this walk would mark the beginning of a lifelong journey.

WALT

It's amazing how two people so different in personality can find so much in common. We didn't meet through friends or family: we just happened to cross paths at the right moment. Looking back, I know it wasn't a coincidence.

The verse from Amos reminds me of that truth: *"Can two walk together unless they agree?"* In other words, can a couple truly walk through life unless their hearts, goals, and values align? For us, the answer was clear — yes.

Some of the vital areas that couples should agree on include things like what kind of activities they like to do, what they want to do in their future, how they want to worship, if they want children, where they would like to live, even what they like to eat. Without some commonalities (agreements) couples may walk together as Amos referenced (choose to marry) and have a long relationship or marriage, but it is unlikely that they will have a relationship (marriage) that is amicable or harmonious.

IKIE

Relationships can't last on feelings alone: they need understanding, patience, and shared faith. From our very first conversation, Walt seemed to value those same things.

WALT

As we spent time together, during the following weeks, I began to see that Ikie wasn't just beautiful; she was strong in spirit. She carried herself with grace and determination. I admired the way she spoke about her family, especially her mother's wisdom and the values she grew up with. It was becoming clear to me that this wasn't just another college romance. I had a feeling in my heart that this was the woman I wanted to build a life with.

We established a friendship that night based on areas that we had in common. We shared enough about ourselves to spark an interest in each other. We became friends, then romantically became involved. Ikie is still my best friend. Our initial friendship was based on commonalities that we recognized in each other's life. Over time, these areas of agreement allowed our courtship to grow and flourish even during the period when we were separated by hundreds of miles.

Although we had a lot of things in common, we were also different in many ways.

***Individual differences
in relationships are important.***

WALT

We cannot deny that often individuals who are opposites in personalities, goals and behaviors tend to be attracted to each other. I am reminded of the individual differences and commonalities of our parents. Mother Lillie, as I affectionately referred to her, was educated, a Christian, quiet, resourceful, and thrifty with spending. She made her little girls' dresses for church from large, washed flour sacks. Mr. Haynes was an uneducated, big talker with "mother wit," outgoing, never meeting a stranger, farmer, Christian, hard-worker and very thrifty with spending. Mr. Haynes and Mother Lillie both desired a home for their family and for their daughters to excel in life.

A similar scenario can be made of the common areas of agreement and differences of my parents. My dad was an educator, farmer, a Christian, a good speaker, and good provider. He was absolutely the "head" of our home. Mama was a great homemaker, a Christian and hard-worker at home and at church. Both of my parents agreed on wanting better homes for our family and they wanted a better future for us than they had.

When Ikie and I started dating (called courting back then), I continued to recognize common areas of agreements that we had, but I discovered some really great differences we had as well. Ikie, had made, for herself, pre-determined reasons for attending Tougaloo, and was singularly focused on her efforts to execute her plans. She knew the path she wanted to take to reach her goals. Ikie was sure of herself, outgoing, and courageous, self-confident, had great self-esteem, was firm in her beliefs and very confident in her skills and abilities. She would not allow distractions to cheat her on the plans she had made for her life. I soon learned that If I wanted to see her, I knew I would need to go to the library or one of the science labs where she would be working on something. At the age of 18 and 19, Ikie was disciplined and organized, completing her papers and projects days or weeks before they were due. Her focus was her **academics.**

I, on the other hand, had come to Tougaloo because I was expected to attend some type of higher learning after high school. It was not necessarily "my idea" but I just knew this was an expectation of my parents. I was not sure about what I wanted to do in my life. At the time I was majoring in biology, with the hope that I would get a teaching job somewhere after graduating. But even that was not a "for sure" outcome or a "for sure" possibility since my minor was in "Bid Whist-ology." You see, while Ikie was studying or experimenting, I was spending most of my time in the student union center playing a card game called "Bid Whist." One would think I thought it was equivalent to having an academic minor in the area of Bid Whist. I loved playing cards, especially that one. On weekends, my buddies and I would play cards all night long at times. It was not unusual, in those days for my buddies and me to pool our meager resources and buy a bottle of cheap wine such as MD-2020 or Thunderbird to sip on while we played cards.

In academic pursuits, Ikie and I were completely opposites. But because of the common areas we shared, our friendship grew into a lasting relationship.

Relationships grow and thrive
when the balance of common areas is balanced
with individual differences.

It is a good thing when a couple has differences that are healthy. Differences do attract and can enhance relationships. Couples can learn and grow from their differences. Ikie's study habits blew my mind. She became an inspiration to me. I started noticing how she responded when she got new assignments. Before we started spending time together, I would get serious about my assignments and projects a week or two or sometimes hours before they were due. While Ikie was calm and collected because her work was done, I was stressed, anxious and working furiously to get mine done on time.

As we continued to grow as a couple, two things began to happen. She began to relax more and gave herself permission to have some fun. Early in the courtship, if I wanted to see her, I would have to go to the science labs to the library or wait outside her dorm until she came. But in time, she would actually come to the student union building occasionally and she learned to play Bid Whist. She got to know my friends and pledged Alpha Kappa Alpha Sorority, Inc. I was already a member of Alpha Phi Alpha Fraternity, Inc. The acceptance of each other's differences enhanced our growing relationship.

Ikie and I are still opposite in many ways. That is normal and expected because we are different people. But over the years, she has taken on more of my character traits in some things, and I have taken on more of hers. Our personalities and behaviors have "blended" over time. We react or respond differently in many circumstances like we did during our college years. So, the question becomes, **"How can a couple who are opposites in individual personalities, behaviors and actions build an effective, lasting, fulfilling relationship that has lasted 62+ years?"** This is a question we have been asked numerous times over the years.

First of all, "differences" should never become "conflicts." We have all heard the phrase, lets agree to disagree.

When individuals disagree, it does not mean that one person is smarter or "more with it" than the other.

Each person's opinions and thoughts about a situation should be explored and discussed in a rational, conversational way, keeping emotions under control. It may be necessary to walk away from the discussion for a "cool down" period before continuing efforts to resolve the issue. Differences of opinions, in our courtship and marriage, have been resolved with the **best possible solution regardless of who presented it**.

When I discovered Ikie's methods of dealing with her studies and we discussed the "why" she did it that way, I was willing to change my modus operandi and get serious about my own goals and aspirations. Sometimes it is necessary to change our positions to achieve the desired outcomes. I wanted to graduate on time, and I wanted to find a job after graduation, so Ikie's way was more beneficial to me. It took no "skin off my nose" to make the changes I needed to make. In fact, eventually, it was to my benefit to make the changes. Later in this book you will see Ikie changing from her behavior on some issues and adopting behaviors I exhibited. A benefit for her was to realize she did not **HAVE** to be studious all the time. She learned that she could have fun and stay on the Dean's List. Today she still has fun playing Bid Whist.

We both recognized that our differences **created a desire to adjust to each other's behaviors.** Ikie could accept where I was and did not attempt, at least overtly, to change me. She permitted me the freedom to make whatever decisions I made on my own, without "nagging" me. I encouraged her to come to the student union building. I wanted her to have those experiences to see another side of college life. I believe that she was happy to see that I saw the need to change my ways on my own. I was happy to see her laughing and having fun. Each of us had to accept the other's feelings and opinions without judgement or criticism. During our marriage, usually, we have experienced respect and appreciation for each other's feelings and behaviors.

In our period of dating and during our years of marriage, we have been transparent in our behavior and communication. This has made our relationship healthy and lasting. Transparency does not mean that partners do not have a right to their own private thoughts. It is important for partners to remember that each of them is an individual, a unique person who has commonalities with their partner **but has** specific different interests and ways of thinking and doing. These differences do not make the partner deceitful or disloyal.

In a marriage or partnership, each person should feel comfortable enough to be honest with the other person and be able to explore other interests without feeling threatened or upset.

Again, difference of opinions on issues should be discussed without lying or trying to hide anything to make either partner "feel good." The best solution should be accepted by both.

When the semester ended that Spring, I knew that I loved Ikie and she loved me. I also wanted to meet her parents. I asked her if I could take her home at the end of the school year. She lived about 65 miles from my home. Neither of us would be students at Tougaloo the following year. I would be teaching, and she would be a nursing student in St. Louis, Missouri, hundreds of miles away. Her parents agreed that I could bring her home, but we must have a chaperone. My father had no problem with that and eagerly accompanied me. This gave him the opportunity to meet Ikie and her parents.

We were pleased that Dad got to meet Ikie's parents. They seemed to like each other. Mr. Haynes and Dad were at ease talking and laughing. Mother Lillie and my dad had both been students at Tougaloo at different times. My dad knew one of Mother Lillie's best friends. All the time we were there, roughly two hours, Ikie and I were dreading the thought of separation. We knew it would be some time before we saw each other again.

REFLECTION AND DISCUSSION QUESTIONS

1. On a scale of 1-10 with 1 being "never" and 10 being "always", at what level do you and your partner have commonalities?

2. What is one difference between you and your spouse that has helped you grow personally or as a couple?

3. How do you and your partner resolve difference in opinions?

4. In your own relationship, how do you practice openness and honesty without losing your individuality?

5. What are some commonalities that you share with your spouse or (partner)? How have they strengthened your relationship?

Chapter 4

MILES APART

"The Lord is close to the broken hearted and saves those who are crushed in spirit."

Psalm 34:18 (NIV)

WALT

During the summer after I graduated, I was blessed to get a job teaching biology at Rogers High School in Canton, Mississippi. During the spring of 1961, I completed the 6-week student-teaching requirement at the same school. I missed the camaraderie of seeing and talking with Ikie. My home from Ikie's home was a little over two hours driving time. I decided to drive back to her home one more time for a bitter/sweet visit later that summer before she left for St. Louis, Missouri.

Teaching was a new experience for me, and I enjoyed class preparations and seeing my students learn. My teaching salary in the first year was $2,900.00. Even though my salary was low, it was the most money I had ever made. That summer, Ikie left for St. Louis.

IKIE

When I left Tougaloo I found myself in a new world. The challenges of college life were over but I soon realized I had new and different challenges. I had been very successful in my academic pursuits during high school and while at Tougaloo. But now I was in a much more academically competitive world. My classmates were young women from across the country. Most had also been superior students in their previous schools. Competing with my new classmates posed my first challenge.

I had been raised in a rural setting and felt ill-equipped to understand many things about urban living. This was another challenge for me. I had to learn to use public transportation since I had no other way to get around the city. My sense of direction then and now is extremely poor, so I got lost a number of times trying to get to a store to shop for personal necessities, groceries and snacks. When I realized I was lost, it was terrifying. I was a farm girl who wasn't used to riding city buses. As an independent young woman, I wanted to learn how to navigate the city on my own and not need to ask others for help.

I found that some of my new classmates were snobbish, unkind, and shallow. Most of them were from large cities and seemed to look at me, coming from Mississippi, as someone who was dumb or slow. Many of them were accustomed to big city nightlife. Some of my classmates were older, divorced women. A few seemed to have come to the school looking for male companionship and husbands. Some frequently would visit nightclubs or bars on Friday and Saturday nights. A few who had left their boyfriends behind soon found reasons to break up with them. They found new love interests. The challenge for me in this scenario was finding true friendships.

I found myself sometimes feeling discouraged but remained firm in the pursuit of my established academic goals to make good grades and learn as much as I could.

First, I knew how proud my daddy was that his baby girl was going to be a registered nurse. Second, I had never given up on anything before and did not want this to be the first. Finally, I had been taught and believed that God was with me and would help me get through this process.

There were times when I thought about leaving. The hospital morgue could be seen from my dorm window. I could also see corpses being taken in and out by ambulance. And at the time, having that proximity with dead people was not anticipated or desired. As time passed, I was assigned a single-occupancy room on the opposite side of the hallway, so I could not see the morgue. Since I did not have a fellow student as a best friend, my ability to vent my feelings was limited. I did most of my venting through my letters to Walt and his phone calls to me.

Being away from home at nineteen in a big city and on my own was a prime opportunity for me to become "wild." In that setting, I could have made some huge mistakes, including being unfaithful to Walt. It was difficult to accept the fact that he was not even in the same state. Thank God, I made a conscious decision. "Being faithful to him would not become an issue for me."

Individuals, in a committed relationship, must find ways to protect it and avoid temptations.

Whenever I considered going against the basic principles Mama taught me at home, I could literally hear her talking, giving life instructions. Her voice would remind me of who I was and the necessity of self-control and self-discipline, regardless of where I was or the circumstances. Another thing that kept me on the straight and narrow and out of trouble was my sincere devotion to Walt. When we talked on the phone or when I wrote him, I never wanted to lie to him about what I was doing. I am thankful to this day for having those guardrails. These guardrails kept me out of trouble and strengthened our relationship.

I missed the professors I had at Tougaloo. They were always available for mentoring and advice whenever I needed it. The instructors at this school were indifferent; you either sank or swam. Students were told during orientation that they had only a few months to attain a certain grade average. If your grades didn't measure up, you were dismissed from school. In other words, the "do or die" rule existed. That academic standard made the learning process highly stressful for most students. The instructors covered a lot of material, and it had to be learned accurately and quickly in a very short amount of time. Within those first few months, some students were forced to leave due to academic failures. My knowledge of the standards was highly stressful for me.

The lectures were long and extremely intense. I had to learn to print the instructor's notes. It was required because nurses' handwritten notes, in those days, had to be printed in patients' charts. My goal at Tougaloo was to always be at the top of my class. At Tougaloo, I was on the Dean's list each semester. I had that same goal at Homer. G. Phillips, but never quite made it to the absolute top of the class. I had good grades, but never the best, despite studying long and hard. I was forced to accept the fact that sometimes our best is not good enough to be the best.

WALT

While Ikie faced many challenges at Homer G. Phillips, I was facing a few of my own. As a first-time teacher, I had to learn how to maintain decorum and control of my class because I had students within four to five years of my age.

Since I could not afford my own apartment and did not have my own transportation, I had to live with my parents. Home was about 13 miles from my work. A fellow teacher, a classmate at Tougaloo, also taught at the school in Canton. He lived about 6 miles closer to the school, in a little town called Farmhaven. I would drive my father's vehicle to his house and carpool with him and his mother. In the evenings, we would reverse the process. This went on for about six months.

When you do not have to pay rent or buy food, $2,900.00 for a school year, seems like a lot of money. Unfortunately, 21-year-olds don't always make wise decisions. A car note was an added challenge to my life. To cut down on some of my expenses, my parents helped me arrange to live closer to my work with a distant great aunt. Even though I was extremely grateful to have a place to sleep and eat and be closer to work, the old house needed a lot of repairs. After I had saved up a little money, I decided I needed my own transportation and bought a new car during the last semester of my first year of teaching.

Walt's mew Chevy Impala

There was a time, while I was living with this aunt, that a skunk got into the house and into my closet. Unfortunately, when my old uncle shot the skunk, it sprayed my clothes including my only sports jacket. I promptly took it to the cleaners hoping to have the scent removed. After I had the jacket cleaned, one morning I wore the jacket to school. While walking down the corridor, I heard some students complaining about the smell of a skunk. I knew immediately that they were smelling my jacket. Apparently, it had not been adequately cleaned. To show my face and prove that I was present, I quickly walked into my classroom, quickly gave an assignment to the class and hurriedly went home. I changed my clothes and returned to school. I was eager to share this fiasco with Ikie, and we shared a great laugh, but I knew that she understood my pain and frustration.

Facing the many challenges which I described above plus the loneliness we both felt, and our inability to see each other face to face, the question must be raised. "How did we manage to keep our relationship vibrant and strong during that extended period of separation?" Our loneliness and separation could have caused us to seek other relationships. If we had, our marriage may not have occurred, and we would not have written this book. We relied on honest, frequent communication to keep our relationship strong.

In long-distance relationships, couples should rely on their mutual love and devotion for each other in order to vent frustrations through whatever forms of communication they use.

Our communications were primarily through writing letters. Ikie would write me more than I wrote her. She would write long frequent letters. I preferred phone calls in lieu of letter writing. I did not like writing letters and as a teacher, I did not have as much time, nor was I as disciplined as Ikie was. I could not afford long phone calls using pay phone booths, so our conversations lasted about five to ten minutes. On my phone calls, I shared with Ikie my frustrations with work, my poor housing conditions and now with a new car, my bills. Ikie did not feel close enough to anyone at her school to share her frustrations with and she did not want to share them with her family. So, she was able to vent through writing me.

Couples should be transparent and supportive with each other in their communication.

I was always eager to hear from her with the hope that I could give her some words of comfort. Despite the miles we were apart, we were able to be supportive of each other's emotional needs.

Maintenance of positive, supportive communication is significantly important when couples are miles apart.

We felt that it was necessary to have an open, honest dialogue when we were able to talk on the phone. And in our letters, we often empathized with each other. Each of us offered advice or made suggestions as much as possible. Sometimes when we were talking on the phone, we would take turns, just listening. There are times when the only comfort one can give is a sympathetic ear. As time passed, with open communication and sensitivity our relationship grew even stronger because we were going through our individual challenges together, as one. In all committed relationships, it is one thing to *say* that you understand, it is another to know that you understand. The partner should know and feel that you understand.

Individuals in a relationship should have the assurance that each is loved and understood even in long distance relationships.

We had to consider that we were miles apart, therefore, it was vital that we find ways to "be there" for each other. We did this by frequently sharing our experiences. There was nothing too insignificant for us to write or talk about. Our goal was to be supportive, encouraging, to show concern and sensitivity during the stresses we faced. These are the behaviors of good friends.

One of the first things I did after buying my new car was drive to St. Louis to visit my sweetheart. Ikie had some distant relatives on Mother Lillie's side who were living in St. Louis. When I visited her, I could stay with one of them. On one of my visits, I asked her to marry me, and she said she would. The next step was to get her parents' approval. We decided that we wanted to marry during her last year of school.

REFLECTION AND DISCUSSION QUESTIONS

1. What are some ways that individual challenges can bring couples closer?

2. Have you had to keep your relationship strong during long separations?

3. What methods did you use to achieve this?

4. What guardrails or boundaries help you and your spouse/partner remain faithful and committed, even when facing challenges or temptations?

5. What are some "small things" you and your spouse share that help you feel close and supported?

Chapter 5

OUR ENGAGEMENT

"He who finds a wife finds a good thing and obtains favor from the Lord."

Proverbs 18:22 (KJV)

WALT

During the middle of Ikie's second year of nursing school, she came home for Christmas. Even though I had visited her in St. Louis during the year, we were looking forward to seeing each other again, face to face, during the Christmas season. It was also somewhat nerve-racking for me because I had planned to ask for Ikie's hand in marriage during that visit. We were of age to make this decision to marry without her parents' consent, but I felt it was important for her parents to agree. We did not want to elope as our parents had. We wanted our parents to feel that we respected them enough to include them in our planning.

I made this very important trip safely and arrived early so I would have time to return home that night. After dinner, Ikie's parents, Ikie, and I were sitting in the family room around the fireplace. Mother Lillie was crocheting as she usually did after dinner. Naturally, I was nervous. It was getting late, around 8:00 p.m. in the evening, and I knew Ikie's mother usually retired to bed relatively early. I continued to get encouragement from Ikie by an occasional intense glance at me accompanied with an enthusiastic nod of her head as if to say, "Go on, ask and get it over."

If possible, a man should ask the father of the potential bride for her hand in marriage.

This showed Ikie's parents that I loved their daughter enough to go through the discomfort of asking for her hand. It also gave Mr. Haynes and me the opportunity to have a meaningful conversation if he desired, about our feelings for each other and of our future.

With an anxious voice and stressful demeanor, I cleared my throat and said, "Mr. Haynes, as you know, Ikie and I have been dating now for about 2 years. Ikie loves me and I love her. We decided that we want to spend the rest of our lives together, so we've decided to get married, and I would like your approval to do so."

Whew, I was so relieved when I got those words out. Mr. Haynes had almost dozed off to sleep. He opened his eyes wide and sat up straighter in his chair and looked intently at me. I was not sure what Mr. Haynes's response would be. I think I subconsciously prepared myself, emotionally, for a negative response. One in which he would say that Ikie should finish school first. It seemed to be a good 3-5 minutes before he finally spoke.

He simply said, "well, if y'all have already decided, I can't say anything that would make any difference. However, I want you to remember this: If you ever have a serious conflict and cannot work it out don't hit her or physically abuse her, just bring her back home."

Physical, mental, verbal, or emotional abuse should never be used to resolve conflicts in marriage or relationships.

Mr. Haynes' comments may have been perceived as out of place at that time and in that setting. But his intention was to prevent any possibility of abuse towards his daughter. His primary concern was about physical abuse because he had seen physical abuse in other people's marriages, including his own family. But abuse in marriages and relationships can take a multitude of forms. Ikie and I have had disagreements on a number of issues but in 62 years, our disagreements have never escalated to abuse. We have always been able to talk about an issue honestly with respect and sensitivity and work it out.

During his comments, I was jarred into remembering how much Ikie meant to Mr. Haynes as his youngest daughter. She had always been his "little boy." I also thought about the fact that Ikie's two older sisters had finished college and worked before either of them had gotten married and there I was asking for Ikie's hand in marriage before she had even finished her education. I had reasons to be anxious.

I have often felt that we were blessed that day. Ikie's parents agreed and supported our decision. Unlike both of our parents who had found it necessary to elope (for different reasons) to get married, Ikie and I had her parents' approval and could begin to plan our future. We were READY to take the next step in our relationship.

Both persons in the relationship should be "ready" for marriage.

Being ready for marriage means that we were willing to put aside our individual preferences for the sake of our relationship. Naturally, I would have preferred my new wife to return to Mississippi with me. But I understood that her goal was to finish school.

I had always known Ikie's values and goals; there was no choice but for her to return to school in Missouri and for me to continue teaching in Mississippi.

Being ready also means that partners take on adult roles in making necessary plans and executing those plans. Ikie has always been a planner, and she had always been determined to execute her plans. She had grown up in a home environment which encouraged achievement and self-confidence. Her dad modeled and encouraged self-confidence in her and her sisters from an early age. He made them believe they could accomplish anything. He wanted his daughters to be independent if necessary.

Another very important characteristic of being "ready" is the ability to be financially independent. Ikie and I had decided that we wanted to be financially independent and not depend on our parents or family members for our financial needs before or after our marriage. We knew that financial independence could be a challenge for us. We would have a small income for my work as a teacher and after graduation and passing state boards Ikie would work as a nurse. With those two sources of income, we felt we would be relatively financially secure.

Young couples getting married should be very frugal with their money, recognizing that most people must learn to crawl before they can walk.

Ikie knew that her parents were not financially able to afford a large expensive wedding for her. She also knew that her older sisters, Selma and Barbara, had been married at their own expense. Ikie did not want her parents to foot the bills for her wedding. She felt compelled to foot most of the bill for her wedding herself. She decided to become a small entrepreneur. She chose to iron uniforms for graduate nurses. Of course, all nurses were required to wear white uniforms that had to be starched and ironed. She charged $.50 for short sleeved uniforms and $.75 for long sleeved uniforms of the graduate nurses who stayed in a separate area of her dorm. She saved monies from her work to purchase material for her wedding dress and her maids of honor. She also purchased my silver wedding band from a pawn shop for $20.00 which I still wear after 62+ years.

Being ready also involves being responsible enough to make wise decisions for yourself and your partner. Some people would not consider marriage before completing their education. That is acceptable. That could be the wisest choice for that couple. Those are choices that couples should make together. Remember that what works for one couple may not be the right decision for someone else. Couples are encouraged to agree on the important issue of when they are ready to move deeper into a committed relationship, engagement, and marriage. We were on the same page and wanted to solidify our relationship with engagement and marriage. We were happy with our decisions about our futures. We did not compare nor were we influenced by anyone when we made our decision to get married. The consequences of our choices could not be placed on anyone else.

That evening ended on a happy note for all of us. We were officially engaged to be married. Before I left for home, I privately placed the ring on Ikie's finger. Somehow, I managed to drive back home. We were now officially engaged. However, both of us knew that in two weeks she would return to Missouri to continue her studies.

REFLECTION AND DISCUSSION QUESTIONS

1. How can couples prepare themselves emotionally and spiritually for marriage?

2. Describe what being ready for marriage means in your own words.

3. How can couples work towards financial independence and stability before and after marriage?

4. How does any form of abuse impact marriage?

5. What are examples of verbal abuse?

Chapter 6

OUR MARRIAGE BEGINS

"For this reason a man will leave his father and mother and be united to his wife, and the two will become one flesh."

Matthew 19:5 (NIV)

IKIE

We chose to get married on August 10, 1963. Our choices for dates to have the wedding were limited because I only had about three weeks before I was to return to Missouri. We planned a simple wedding on the lawn of my parents' home. In Mississippi, the months of July and August are the hottest months of the year. Some days it was blistering hot with very few breezes. During the 1950s and 60s, very few Black people in our areas had air conditioning, in fact, not many cars had it. Your family was doing pretty good if you had window fans in your home, which produced quite a bit of warm air based upon what speed you selected the rotary blades to turn. That was certainly better than not having a fan.

I had saved enough money from ironing uniforms of graduate nurses at my school to purchase material for my wedding dress, the maids of honor, and a small trousseau that she would use during our two-week honeymoon in Gary, Indiana. We had a small reception in the dining room of my home. The food was very modest and simple, consisting of cookies, finger sandwiches, punch, and a wedding cake which was made by my sister, Barbara.

Couples should keep their wedding and reception expenses within their financial capabilities.

In my opinion, the couple who takes greater ownership for their wedding are more committed to making the marriage work. So many couples spend thousands on huge weddings only to get divorced in a few years or less.

Daddy borrowed metal chairs from a local funeral home. He also made an altar that the minister stood in the back of with our rustic, brown cornfield in the background, and he made a kneeler and placed it in front the lectern. Mama padded and covered it for us to kneel during the prayer. I made a few hundred paper carnations from colored facial tissue which I used to decorate the altar and for reserved chairs for family members. Walt and his best man had rented tuxedos. He managed to buy the boutonnieres for himself and the other groomsmen.

WALT

We repeated our wedding vows at 2:00 p.m. It was a hot muggy day. The temperature had to have been in the mid-90's with 90% humidity. It was so hot that most of the gathered guests chose to stand rather than sit in the hot chairs. Even though it was extremely hot and uncomfortable, Ikie and I listened with our hearts and minds to the vows we were making to each other, and before God.

Each of us said, **"I take thee to be my wedded wife (husband).** This was our free will. It was not a forced marriage. To us "wedded" meant we were becoming spiritually, emotionally and physically connected.

Wedding vows promote couples to teammate status for a lifelong journey.

Then we said, **"To have and to hold from this day forward."** The verb, "to have" means that united couples have the freedom to enjoy deeper relationships including sexual relationships. Further, it means that couples should strive to understand and know their partner.

***Understanding and knowing your partner
begins with friendship. Friendship is based on a
number of things including respect and trust.***

We became friends during our college days. We understood each other through a number of ways including communication, honesty, emotional support, and empathy. Our friendship became our courtship, and our courtship led us to our marriage. "To hold" means that we promised to take care of or watch out for each other from that day on.

We vowed that our union was, **"For better, for worse, for richer, for poorer, in sickness and in health."** This is a promise to stay faithful and committed no matter what happens. Over these 62+ years Ikie and I have needed each other during our up times, down times, good times, bad times, sicknesses, surgeries, and everything in between. Every time one of us had to face a difficult issue the other one is there to lean on. As scripture says, *"The two shall become one,"* our marriage has become stronger because we journey through life together.

***It is easier to face challenges in marriage
when the couple faces them as ONE.***

We promised **"to love and to cherish."** Love involves sacrifice. "To cherish" means that partners are stating that they recognize the marvelous value of their spouse not only as God's creation but also as a human being created in God's image.

Partners should be willing to give up something they want for the sake of their partner.

You will see in the next chapter that Walt was willing to leave Mississippi and move to Illinois because I did not want to come back to Mississippi. Because of the nature of Walt's work as a minister and chaplain over the years, I sacrificed having a career that I envisioned and had great hopes of achieving. Although I did not achieve my earlier goals, I achieved so much more by being able to travel to many parts of the world, places, and experiences I could never have imagined in my wildest dreams. Both of us loved and cherished each other so much that we were each willing to give up something we wanted for harmony in our marriage.

The last part within the vow—**"till death do us part"**— is a very difficult concept for many couples today. When these words are spoken, an implied agreement is made between the couple. With this vow we were saying that death would be the only thing that would dissolve our marriage. Some people cannot imagine staying married to the same person for the rest of their life. We have remembered this vow. We encourage couples to remember that they made this commitment before man but more importantly before God.

Couples should make every effort possible to honor their marriage vows.

IKIE

Traditional wedding vows have been used in marriages for many years. Some couples rewrite the original words and make them into their own. Many couples find that they don't appreciate the meaning of their wedding vows until they have been married for long periods.

BEAMONS' 50TH ANNIVERSARY

PHOTOS BY BRIAN HUGHES | News Bulletin

Ikie and Chaplain Col. (retired) Walter Beamon celebrated their 50th anniversary Saturday at Hurlburt Field's Soundside Club. **INSIDE:** Also celebrating an anniversary are the Millers, who have been married 69 years. Read their story on **A2.**

Beaming after 50 years

Retired Air Force chaplain, local minister and wife celebrate golden anniversary

"She had told God she would have anyone he sent her but she didn't want a preacher ... and then came this guy who couldn't even dance fast."

Oledia Bell, Master of Ceremonies

By BRIAN HUGHES
682-6524 | @cnbBrian
brianh@crestviewbulletin.com

HURLBURT FIELD — Chaplain Col. (retired) Walter and Ikie Beamon celebrated their golden anniversary Saturday at the Hurlburt Field Soundside Club surrounded by more than 250 family members and friends.

The Beamons and their guests were serenaded by The Wesley Boys gospel harmony quartet, the First United Methodist Church of Crest-view bell choir, and a solo rendition of "The Lord's Prayer" performed by Dorothy Washington of Shaw Temple A.M.E. Zion Church in Atlanta.

See 50 YEARS A7

First United Methodist Church bell choir members perform a patriotic medley during the Beamons' anniversary party.

BRIAN HUGHES | News Bulletin

50 YEARS from page A1

Col. Beamon is a retired former associate pastor at First United Methodist, where the Sunday school class instructed by the couple is the largest in the church.

The evening's Master of Ceremonies, the Rev. Oledia Bell, said the couple met at a school dance at Tougaloo College in Mississippi during Ikie Beamon's sophomore year.

"She had told God she would have anyone he sent her but she didn't want a preacher ... and then came this guy who couldn't even dance fast," Bell said.

Walter Beamon graduated with a biology degree in 1960 and taught school for several years. He graduated from the Virginia Union School of Theology in 1969.

Ikie Beamon, a retired registered nurse, followed her husband when, as the Air Force Chaplains Service's ninth black chaplain in its 69-year history, he was transferred to South Korea.

During Saturday's celebration, Chaplain Col. (ret.) Robert Jemerson, senior pastor at Second Baptist Church in San Antonio, led the Beamons in renewing their wedding vows.

As church and Air Force friends offered tributes to the couple, Chaplain Col. (ret.) John Blair likened the Beamons to TV's Jeffersons.

"Since they were from Mississippi, they had their piece of the pie, but unlike the Jeffersons, fish would fry in their kitchen and beans would burn on their grill," Blair said to laughter.

While thanking their guests for sharing in their celebration, Pastor Beamon offered some advice for a long, happy marriage.

"The best way to stay married this long is to learn this phrase: 'Yes, dear,'" he said.

As the evening concluded and guests departed, "Movin' On Up," "The Jeffersons" theme song, played over the sound system.

FIND IT ONLINE

See www.crestviewbulletin.com/news/community for a photo gallery of the Beamons' anniversary celebration and a link to a video tribute.

On August 10, 2013, at 2:00 pm, Walt and I renewed our wedding vows during our 50th wedding anniversary. I am eternally grateful to God that we took our wedding vows seriously when we were married, but I must admit they meant more to us fifty years later.

As I mentioned at the beginning of this chapter, when we got married the heat was almost unbearable. Because of the heat I was glad when the brief ceremony was over. It was nice to be in the shade and have something cool to drink at our little reception. It's hard to say who compensated the late Reverend A.D. Gray who performed our wedding ceremony, Walt, or my daddy. After nearly 62 years, some details have unfortunately faded from memory. It was important to us to ensure that the reverend was compensated.

WALT

Earlier, that year, I had secured a summer job in Gary, Indiana. Ikie and I stayed with a family friend who lived in Gary for two weeks after our wedding. We called that our honeymoon. When the two weeks ended, Ikie went back to St. Louis to finish her education, and I returned home to my teaching position. It was a difficult nine months for us, but we tried to see each other as often as possible. I spent long hours driving to Missouri and Ikie came home when she could. Both of us remained faithful to our marriage vows, even though both or either could have broken the vows during our separation and no one perhaps would have ever known, except God. Satan always tests us at our weakest link. Temptation comes in many forms, but the Bible is clear that we can resist it if we really are determined. Listen to the apostle Paul in speaking to the church of Corinth.

> *"No temptation has seized you except what is common to man. And God is faithful; He will not let you be tempted beyond what you can bear. But when you are tempted, He will also PROVIDE an escape, so that you can stand up under it."*

> 1 Corinthians 10:13 (ESV)

One thing is certain, temptation is inevitable in all our lives, but God is faithful in providing a way of escape through the empowerment of the Holy Spirit. We can endure and overcome.

Mignon McLaughlin, a journal and author, made this observation about marriage *which both of us agree w*ith.

"A successful marriage requires falling in love many times, and always with the same person."

H. Norman Wright had this poignant saying:

"In a good marriage the husband and wife are friends. Friendship means companionship, communication, and co-operation. This is known as philia."

King Solomon, in speaking to his sons brings it all home in saying,

> *"The man who finds a wife finds a treasure and receives favor from the Lord."*
>
> Proverbs 18:22 (NIV)

REFLECTION AND DISCUSSION QUESTIONS

1. Which part of the traditional wedding vows stands out most to you, and why?

2. What role does friendship play in building a lasting marriage?

3. What does it mean to face challenges 'as one', and how can that mindset strengthen a marriage?

Chapter 7

NEW REVELATIONS

*"Call me and I will answer you and tell you great and
unsearchable things you do not know."*

Jeremiah 33:3 (NIV)

WALT & IKIE

Someone once said, "Every man wants a beautiful wife, a smart wife, a loving wife, and a cooperative wife, Sadly, polygamy is against the law."

There are always surprises in relationships when newly married couples start living together every day. They begin to see behaviors they had not seen before and to hear beliefs or stories they had not heard before.

Perhaps these surprising revelations are the primary reasons that many couples choose to "test the waters" by living together before committing to marriage. Their attitude seems to imply, "If my partner's behaviors and values are SO conflicted with mine that it's difficult to live with them, then I certainly don't want to marry him/her."

Our response to their way of thinking is with these questions: First, do you really love the person? Second, do you have to know every little thing about them to have a healthy marriage? Third, are you willing to do the work needed to work through differences to have a healthy, positive relationship? Your answers to these questions should give you some directions about the future of the relationship.

Because of our personal feelings on the issue of living together versus getting married, Walt and I chose to marry first. Not only was our decision to marry based on our personal convictions but also on the role modeling of our parents and other extended family members. While growing up, we saw those "old folks" work out their differences or conflicts. It was not always easy. Both partners had to learn that partnership meant "sometimes compromising" to achieve the best outcome.

When we agreed to marry, we believed we could face challenges or climb any mountain together. Our first few years of living together revealed several surprises about each other. In this chapter, we will share some of the challenges we faced and how we worked to find solutions.

WALT

After Ikie completed her education, we had to decide what our next step would be. One major concern was where we wanted to live. I had never lived more than a couple of months anywhere except Madison County, Mississippi. This was my home, where my parents and extended family lived. Plus, this is where I was employed. I was comfortable in Mississippi. Beyond that, as my parents' only son, I believed that my parents expected me to come back, help with farm work and be available for them as they aged.

IKIE

I had lived in St. Louis, for three years. My experiences and exposures had been very different from those I remembered in Mississippi.

Ikie's Graduation from Nursing School

Also, I believed there were few, if any, African Americans registered nurses in the state of Mississippi at that time. I felt that my chances for finding work in my career field as an RN were slim. The main reason I had gone to Homer G. Phillips, in St. Louis, was because there were no schools for African American women to become registered nurses in the state of Mississippi. I was appalled with the thought of returning to the state of Mississippi. That was not what I wanted to do.

WALT

I was torn between her desires and those of my own. We had to have a serious conversation about this situation. We literally listed the positives and negatives of returning to Mississippi and those we would have by leaving the state. My future employment in Mississippi was a relatively sure thing; I already had a job. But Ikie did not, and she was correct in thinking that her chances for getting employment as a registered nurse in the state were limited.

I also thought about the fact that at 23 years of age I had basically been living in the same general area, never really living far from my home and family. Then I started thinking about how I might grow as a person if we relocated somewhere else. I would have opportunities to experience new and different things in a completely new environment. We could start our lives together and conquer the world.

IKIE

I was not set on a particular place to live; I just didn't want to come back to Mississippi. After a lengthy discussion, we mutually agreed to leave the state. That was the solution that worked best for us. In July of 1964, we put all our belongings in the trunk of our car and headed to Chicago, Illinois.

WALT

Chicago was the most logical place for us for several reasons. First, it was near Gary, Indiana, where two of my sisters and some distant relatives lived. The thought of having loved ones near was comforting for both of us. Second, we knew a couple, whom we had known in college and were colleagues of mine, who were living there. They had relocated to Chicago. When we decided for sure that we were not going back to Mississippi, I applied for a teaching position in biology in the public school system and was accepted. I was to begin working roughly two weeks after our arrival in the city.

IKIE

I had taken my state board licensing tests and was awaiting the results. I applied to Michael Reese Hospital for a position as staff nurse on a medical/surgical floor. While waiting for my test scores, I was employed by the hospital as a graduate nurse. Later that fall, I was elated to be informed that I was successful in passing the Missouri State Boards. I had passed all five areas of testing which officially promoted me from a graduate nurse to a registered nurse. Since my education was an affiliated program between Tougaloo and Homer G. Phillips, when I completed nursing education and became a RN, I also received a B.S. degree in Biology from Tougaloo.

Later in our marriage, after Walt entered the United States Air Force, I attended The Peabody Vanderbilt Overseas Program and received a Master of Arts in Human Development Counseling.

When we say that we put everything we owned in the trunk of our car, we are being literal. We had our clothes, some bath towels, and cloths, four plates, six forks, spoons, and knives, two sets of regular bed sheets and a couple of quilts that my mother had made and given us. We also had a few dish cloths/towels, a small and a medium size cooking pot. The day we moved into our apartment our friends loaned us a card table with four chairs.

Walt at our apartment building

That is where we sat and ate. A couple that they knew loaned us a twin size bed to sleep on until we were financially able to buy furniture for our home.

WALT

I started in my new job two weeks after we moved into our apartment. Until Ikie got her license, she had worked as a graduate nurse. The pay grade difference for graduate nurses versus registered nurses was significant. We were both employed. Both of us contributed to our household budget. Our incomes allowed us to gradually improve our standard of living.

Both partners in marriage should contribute to the household budget if possible.

Some couples have "old money." Old money means they are very well off financially and have parents or other relatives who augment their financial needs. They don't need to rely on their incomes. However, for the average couple, including us, both partners should be willing to work to support the household.

We gradually got into a daily routine that was comfortable for us. Since we had just one car, I would drop Ikie off at her work and drive on to mine. Sometimes Ikie would use the city transit if I had problems picking her up. We would work all week and rest and have fun on weekends.

I enjoyed the changes Chicago provided in contrast to the life I had known in Madison County. The city was a busy, busy place. I learned how to drive in the worst traffic jams. On Friday and Saturday nights we would go "clubbing", going from one club to another, or playing cards, one of my favorite activities with newfound friends. Those were not activities we would have done back home. We were not attending church anywhere. We felt we were truly grown-up and did not consider our parents' teachings or their role modeling. We had left home and on our own.

Ikie was trying hard to fulfill her role as a working wife who could successfully juggle our social lives, her job as a staff nurse, and our home, including cooking. Most of her meals were mediocre at best. I had not complained but I had begun to miss my mother's good cooking. It was becoming increasingly apparent that her cooking was not her strongest suit.

Thanksgiving was on the horizon the following November. She had never cooked a Thanksgiving meal before. She had seen her mother cook fat hens for Thanksgiving with dressing and all the other fixings typical for dinner on that holiday. Although I had been having difficulty with her meals, I had never mentioned this fact to her. Her inability to cook was a new revelation to me. In fact, we had not discussed cooking at all. I assumed that she could cook before we were married because she grew up in rural Mississippi and had two older sisters who could cook, and her mother was an exceptional cook. I had not been transparent about how I was feelings, and my dissatisfaction was growing.

One day she struck up a conversation with one of our neighbors about what the neighbor was preparing for Thanksgiving. The neighbor informed Ikie that she was cooking a duck. This intrigued her. Ikie has always been adventurous and eager to try something new and different. She asked the neighbor about how to cook a duck. The neighbor proceeded to explain that it was a simple process. She instructed Ikie to take the duck out of its wrapping paper, wash it and season it. After seasoning the duck, she should put it in the oven, preheated to 350 degrees. Then she should multiply the number of pounds that the duck weighed by 30 minutes to determine how long the duck should cook. It will be delicious, she told Ikie. Ikie purchased a frozen duck from our local grocery store and put it in the freezer.

On Thanksgiving morning, Ikie excitedly removed the duck from the freezer and prepared the duck exactly as she had been instructed. My stomach was grumbling in anticipation of a wonderful Thanksgiving meal, especially with the neighbor giving Ikie instructions on how to cook the duck. When we sat down to eat, I was salivating after saying grace and started to carve this beautifully browned duck. When I tried to penetrate it with a knife, it was not only tough as leather, but blood squirted out and pooled from the penetration of the knife where I had stuck it. It was apparent that the duck was undercooked. Our neighbor had failed to mention that the duck should be thawed for several hours before putting it into the oven and Ikie did not know that. Needless to say, my day was ruined and I had to count to ten, take some deep breaths and suggest that we get some burgers from a popular burger joint for our dinner. Both of us were upset about the "duck meal." When things went wrong with Thanksgiving dinner, we should not have lost our heads, the duck had already done that for us.

The question of who's at fault in this scenario can be raised. I was unaware that her experience as a cook had been so limited. But during the next few days I learned that Ikie never had to cook when she was back home because she had two older sisters who did the cooking. She had spent her early years doing things with her dad. I remembered that she had been her dad's little boy.

Newly married couples should expect to learn new things about their spouse when they live together.

This was a revelation that I had not realized before we were married. To add fuel to the fire, I was a finicky eater. I was accustomed to my mother's "good cooking." We had to have another serious conversation.

IKIE

I recognized that my cooking skills were limited. This was a challenge for both of us. I did not want Walt to be upset with me because of the meals I prepared. I was determined to learn how to cook to please him. He seemed determined to give me the time I needed to improve.

> **When a problem in a marriage exists,**
> **both partners should make every effort to solve**
> **the problem as soon as possible.**

WALT

Ikie had trust and respect for me and wanted me to be happy eating the meals she prepared. Partners in a marriage should possess a desire to "make it right" as much as possible for each other. In other words, if healthy relationships are to thrive each person must want the other person to be happy. Perhaps the main reason I had not been transparent about how I felt about her cooking before was because I was trying to make her happy by eating the food she had been preparing. We should have had a conversation about it much sooner.

When I reacted to the uncooked duck by suggesting that we get a burger for dinner, Ikie could have taken a position of defiance. She could have been angry, hurt or retaliated with angry words or behavior. Instead, she humbly accepted the truth that she was not a good cook, and failed at cooking a good Thanksgiving dinner. Taking a position of defiance about the important issue of not being able to cook was not an option for her. She was unashamed. In this critical case she did not mind seeking help to work on the issue. She took the initiative to reach out to her mother and two sisters for help. Her mother and sisters would send simple recipes by mail. Her parents had a telephone, so she called home to ask questions and get instructions. She would find recipes in magazines or books and try them out on me. Some of them were great, some not so much.

Every time she was successful with a new dish her confidence in her cooking skills grew. I recognized that learning to cook, as with any other skill, takes time and practice. I was willing to be patient and give her the opportunity to improve her cooking skills. Because of my patience and Ikie's persistence, over the weeks, months, and years she has become an excellent cook. We worked through this issue together and avoided a potential problem.

A couple of years earlier while teaching back in Mississippi, I considered myself to be a very good teacher. I was never the greatest teacher, but I enjoyed making lesson plans and exposing my students to as much related information as I could. Here, in Chicago, I continued to make lesson plans, but my interest was not at the same level as it had been. The students didn't seem to be motivated to learn as much as my classes in Mississippi. As I reflect on it now, perhaps I was not as engaged as I had been earlier. There were gangs in the area of the school and there were other distractions from schoolwork.

I developed an interest in photography. This was a surprise to Ikie and me. I found myself spending as much time with that hobby as I did with my classwork. I took pictures of skylines, buildings, stars, flowers and learned to develop them in darkness in our bathroom tub. This went on for several months, but that interest began to gradually fade. I met a guy who liked to fish, so I picked that up as a hobby. Both of these hobbies were expensive. Recently, while we were writing this book I read a profound statement about money, **"They say money talks,"** but during that time, mine just waved goodbye. I suppose I felt I could spend more money because we were making more money than we ever had before. Since the money I used to support these hobbies came from our general household budget, I should have had a conversation with Ikie about doing them before starting them. Of course, this is all in hindsight.

Couples get into trouble with money when they keep things from each other such as secret purchases and other purchases made without mutual agreement that impact the household budget.

For some married couples, keeping boundaries around separate piles of money works best for them. For others, a "what's mine is mine and what's yours is mine" is an approach which doesn't usually work very well. It is more desirable that couples come to an agreement on spending habits that affect their budget.

Spending money freely was not a problem for me. It did not bother me to use a credit card for purchases and only pay the minimum amount due each month. But I found out that paying only the minimum monthly amount would get me into trouble later! I found that after twelve months my balance was practically the same as when the purchases were made.

My dad was well known in our town and community. He could walk into a bank and get a loan with just his verbal promise to pay it back, which he always did. I remember one year he purchased a new car and a truck during the same year while two of my sisters were in college. He managed to pay all his bills when they became due and to my knowledge, he was never in financial trouble. I figured that I could do something similar. My approach to spending money was to live life fully and pay expenses as they arose. I felt that the bills would eventually get paid. I was stuck between the mentalities of "I need to save money" and "you only live once."

IKIE

Spending money, without proper planning, was a serious problem for me. I grew up in a home where every dollar our household spent was planned. Although we were not rich, my parents paid cash for almost everything they bought. They identified their goals to buy a particular item and a time frame to save for it. To this we had to sacrifice other things.

Mama would patch her dresses and Daddy's overalls. We had one pair of shoes for working in the field and a pair for Sunday. Mama could sew and would wash and bleach flour sacks. They could make our Sunday dresses without a pattern. She did that throughout our young years. Most of our food came from our farm so we did not spend much money buying food. The primary food we bought included flour, sugar, and coffee. So, they were able to save until they had enough cash to make the purchase.

When my parents decided to build a new bigger house, they paid for most of it in cash. They would save enough to buy so many windows and store them in a shed. Then, save enough to buy doors and store them in the shed, etc. When they started building the house, they purchased most of the lumber and other materials and had paid cash for them.

WALT

Obviously, the issue of how to handle money was a problem in our marriage, especially since we pooled our money together. Over the years I have usually been the partner who spent, and Ikie has been the one that economized. Somehow through compromises and conversation, we have made it work. Either she would convince me that we did not need something, or I would convince her that we did. I was better at convincing her to spend money than she was at convincing me not to.

She told me that I missed my true calling. Because I could find ways to justify my spending, she said I should have been a lawyer. To offset my spending habits, Ikie started budgeting. This ensured that our most important bills were paid. I learned to plan my spending better from recognizing the benefits of planning and budgeting. We were able to pay our bills and save money.

Ikie pondering our budget

Sensitivity to each other's desires with communication and compromise helps couples solve financial problems.

Couples should discuss their differences and opt for the solution that suits them best. As a result of budgeting, I became astute in paying off my credit card bills monthly, so we would not accrue any interest charges.

I met a chemistry teacher at my school. I am going to refer to him as "Al." His classroom was adjacent to mine. I taught biology. Having a common interest in science, we soon became good friends. He was a godly man who was full of the Holy Spirit. I started to digest what he shared, and I really began to hear his strong dynamic spiritual testimony. During our conversations, I discovered that he had a kind of peace that I had desired. We talked frequently about his spiritual life and how becoming a follower of Christ had changed his life.

Al gave me books to read and scriptures that had been helpful to him in becoming a committed follower of Jesus Christ. As time passed, I began to have new and different thoughts about my life and my future. I found pleasure in prayers and devotional readings. I did not recognize that I was also beginning to make behavioral changes.

My hobbies of photography and fishing became less important to me. I also found less time to do lesson plans and prepare for my classes. I found myself becoming more interested in reading books written by pastors, subscribing to and reading religious magazines, and listening to Christian music.

On the day of my conversion experience in my classroom, I was led to purchase a Bible. I went to Sears Roebuck and purchased a King James version. I found myself reading the Bible more and cross-referencing verses.

Walt's behavior changes

Sometimes Ikie would find me sound asleep late at night in the recliner with the Bible opened in my lap. I received Jesus Christ as my personal Savior during this time.

IKIE

I started noticing changes in Walt's behavior. Because of the several new hobbies he had taken up recently, I thought this new religious focus was just another interest. I did not put too much stock in it. I racked it up as "just another hobby." In the meantime, I decided to start taking some education courses at a local college. I was considering teaching, because first, I enjoyed teaching patients during the few opportunities I had at work and because I was tired of the required rotation through three different shifts every four to six weeks as a staff nurse. My classes were three nights a week, which I attended after I got home from work.

WALT

We met several of our neighbors, most were congenial and friendly. However, there was a beautiful young single mother, approximately in her early thirties. I am going to call her "Joan." Joan confided in me that she had a number of issues with her ex-husband. He was not emotionally or financially supportive of her or their 4-year-old daughter. Joan was an elementary school teacher in the Illinois Public School System, but her income was barely enough to meet the needs of her child and herself. She had filed for child support through the legal system and was waiting for the judicial process to be completed. I genuinely felt sorry for her. I thought about the fact that any one of my four sisters could have been in this young woman's situation. As a new Christian, overwhelmingly desiring to help others find peace in their lives, I felt it was my duty to be supportive and help her find some joy and peace in her apparently troubled life. I wanted to share my faith in Jesus Christ with her. I literally took the part of the Bible about "bearing fruit" to heart and was determined to bring some changes in Joan's life for the better.

I got Joan's permission to share her situation with Al at work. Al and I decided to follow biblical teaching and help this young woman find Christ. We visited her several times in her home. We discussed salvation and shared our beliefs with her. She eagerly listened to us and appeared to want the peace we had. Since I lived in the same complex as her, I had the opportunity to talk with her frequently. She read the books I loaned her, and then she and I would talk about them. When she invited me to dinner and did not invite Ikie, I should have had a clue that her responses to my attention may not have been related to what I thought they were. Perhaps she had other motives in mind.

> *"There is a way that seems right to a man, but in the end, it leads to their destruction."*
>
> Proverbs 14:12 (NIV)

REFLECTION AND DISCUSSION QUESTIONS

1. Why do you think some couples choose to live together before marriage?

2. What are the potential benefits and risks?

3. What new revelations or surprises did you discover about your spouse after marriage?

4. What are some healthy ways couples can manage money together?

5. How do you see God using unexpected challenges to strengthen marriages?

Chapter 8

TEMPTATIONS, TESTS AND TRIALS

When tempted, no one should say, "God is tempting me."
For God cannot be tempted by evil, nor does He tempt
anyone;

James 1:13 (NIV)

WALT & IKIE

We've all heard the question, "Which came first the chicken or the egg?" Since one leads to another, in an endless cycle, the question is hard to answer. We might also ask a similar question from a human perspective "Which comes first–a test or a temptation?" We could go further and ask the question, "What is the difference between a test and a temptation? In response, we should think of these terms in this way: A trial can lead to temptation; a temptation can become a test. And temptations and tests can become, if prolonged, trials. This chapter will deal with what we are calling the "Joan Event" in our marriage. The Joan Event, for us, represents a temptation which became a test and a trial that we were eventually able to overcome. It also shows that inexperience can potentially lead to great mistakes.

WALT

Over the years, during my ministry and in just dealing with people, I have discovered that many men are often naive when interacting with women. A naïve person is one who lacks worldly experience and understanding. He or she is too willing to believe that someone is telling the truth, that people's intentions in general are good, or that life is simple or fair. Most of the time people are naïve because they are young and have not had much experience in life. That was the case with my dealing with Joan. I believed she needed my counseling and emotional support. It never occurred to me while interfacing with her that she had any ulterior motives.

Ikie and I had become involved in a local church in the city. I had been encouraging Joan to come to the church for fellowship. I thought being with other Christians would help strengthen her faith. She did come on several occasions. On one of those Sundays, I rendered a solo with the choir. During the selection I was surprised when she appeared to have been "overcome" by the Holy Spirit. I was pleased that she was moved and thanked God that she was accepting His salvation.

The church celebrated an annual Men's Day program as a fund-raiser. All the men of the church were asked to contribute $100.00. Joan heard about it and volunteered to contribute half of mine, $50.00. I simply thought she was being generous and gracious. This also surprised me because she had shared her lack of adequate income.

One evening I decided to surprise Ikie by cleaning our apartment while she was at school. I had gone out to empty some trash. The trash dumpster was located at the rear of our apartment building at the back of Joan's bedroom. Two sets of bedroom windows allowed a clear view of the dumpster, so she was able to see me when I went to empty the trash. I heard her open her window. Then she called my name. When I turned to look, I saw that she was leaning out the window, braless and wearing a see-through negligee. I looked away immediately, and she started a conversation completely contrary to the "being saved" conversations we had recently been having. The tone and the content of her conversation at that time made me extremely uncomfortable. It was very inappropriate.

My personality may be considered "gentle." By this, I mean that I am kind, mild, and unruffled by nature. I have always been considerate of others and treat them with respect and empathy. I am generally non-confrontational, preferring to resolve conflicts in a peaceful and diplomatic manner. I had considered myself as only being supportive to this neighbor who had shared her very sad and abusive history with me. I wanted to be polite but also at this moment, I wanted to just get away. At that moment Ikie drove up. I dreaded the conversation I knew we were going to have.

IKIE

As a child I frequently foresaw events. Walt said, this is called discernment. I remember one time I asked Daddy not to put pine kindling on the fire in the fireplace. The kindling was from a pine stump that dynamite had been used to dislodge it from the ground. He ignored me

95

and residue from the dynamite blew up a portion of the house. He was injured. Mama and I were blown on the opposite side of the room. Another time I recall telling Mama and my sisters to "let's go inside the house" during a rainstorm. Immediately as we got up to leave lightning struck the antenna that we had been sitting near on the porch. So, I guess I had a gift to sense when things were threatening.

One evening while at one of my classes, I had a sudden, overwhelming urge to leave my class and come home. I seemingly could not force myself to stay in class. That was most unusual for me because I enjoyed learning. When I drove up to our apartment complex and observed Joan, I was appalled at what I saw.

I had been raised in the church, and my parents were strong Christians. I had been very tolerant of Walt's friendship with Joan as I felt a "good" wife would be. I had seen the interactions between Joan and Walt, and I did not feel comfortable with their friendship, probably because I was excluded.

A few days earlier, in an effort to ease the tension I felt. I casually said to Walt, "I am unhappy that you are spending so much time with Joan; she barely speaks to me. I think she has more on her mind than religion and salvation." His response was something like, "In my conversations with her, I have discovered that she has several challenging problems. Joan is a sad soul who needs help, and I'm simply trying to help her. I feel this is what God wants me to do. I think she is beginning to accept Jesus as her Savior, and that is my goal. I responded, **"If your relationship with Joan continues as it has been I will have to leave you.** She seldom speaks to me or responds when I speak to her." He replied, **"If I have to choose between you and my God, I will choose**

my God.” I responded, **“Well if it continues, I’ll leave you right here with Joan and your God!”**

WALT

As I walked from the dumpster back to our apartment. I felt remorseful because my interactions with Joan had been misinterpreted. I was ashamed that I had not recognized Joan’s intentions, and I felt fearful that I had inadvertently damaged our marriage.

Although I was not guilty of anything that would put our marriage in jeopardy, I felt I was caught between a rock and a hard place. Ikie got out of the car, did not speak and headed straight to the apartment. Even though I was so thankful that she came home, I knew our marriage was being tested and I dreaded having the conversation we had to have.

Satan uses weak moments and minds by attempting to manipulate us into sinful behaviors. There are numerous tests and trials we can draw from this example of a critical event in our marriage: Satan had used Joan to tempt me into a situation that could potentially permanently damage our marriage. He had used Al and me because we were vulnerable as naïve men, eager to help a fellow human who we perceived was in trouble. Satan could have used Ikie.

The fact that she kept control during a contentious situation showed her maturity. Ikie had never seen evidence that I was unfaithful. She was able to keep her head because she knew I loved her and had always been faithful.

Faithfulness in marriage is vital in
maintaining a healthy relationship.

Infidelity in marriage is defined as one losing trust or breaking a promise to remain faithful to a partner or spouse.

Any action that violates an agreement between two people and harms their relationship is considered infidelity. There are a multitude of reasons for infidelity. Included in these are: inability to communicate effectively; boredom, feeling unwanted or unappreciated, revenge, and unfulfilled sexual desires. Unfulfilled sexual desires can result in indiscriminate lust even for someone else's wife.

King Soloman gave his young son some sound advice related to involvement with other women. This same advice could be given to a daughter as well. I have reflected on this passage a few times over the years when I have counseled couples who are preparing to marry. I suggested that they heed his advice.

> *"My son, pay attention to my wisdom: listen carefully to my wise council. For the lips of an immoral woman are sweet as honey, and her mouth is smoother than oil. But in the end she is bitter as poison, and as dangerous as a double-edged sword."*
>
> Proverbs 5:1-4 (NLT)

He goes on to say:

> *"Don't lust for her beauty. Don't let her coy glances seduce you."*
>
> Proverbs 6:25 (NIV)

Couples must always be on guard to avoid falling into the traps of unscrupulous people they will encounter in life.

Proverbs is a book in the Bible providing wisdom on many subjects. The wisdom shared about the behaviors in marriages is vital to understand and obey in order to maintain healthy marriages. This is the kind of wisdom that Ikie and I learned to follow after our Joan event. We have followed these instructions throughout our marriage to this day. We have avoided circumstances that might put our devotion to each other in jeopardy. This kind of wisdom comes with age and experience. We pray that younger married couples will gain this wisdom from these instructions. Remember that some people will **plot** ways to destroy happy marriages.

When married individuals yield to temptations, they have committed adultery. *Adultery is a sin, regardless of which gender yields to it.* After all, adultery takes two people or one with power over the other, at the very least. The goal of married people is to avoid yielding to the temptation of "greener grass" on the other side of the fence.

I prayed as I began that dreaded conversation. Thank God when we talked, we were both emotionally mature enough to keep our composure, but the atmosphere was tense and uncomfortable. With humility, I reminded Ikie of the reasons I had reached out to Joan in the first place. It was not my intention to develop a personal relationship. I simply wanted to help Joan find Christ and have peace.

IKIE

There were several factors which helped me deal successfully with very strong feelings about the Joan event. I had seen Walt's behavioral changes related to Christian spirituality, so I knew he had based his actions on trying to fulfill what he thought were Christian obligations. I felt his actions were pure because he is naturally very sympathetic and empathetic towards anyone he perceives is in need. I never felt our marriage was really threatened.

> *Individuals who are secure in their relationship should not be threatened by mistakes of their spouse, instead, remember who you married and why.*

God provided a way for Walt to have a "wake up" call. God was the reason I had that sudden urge to come home that day at that time. I understood and believed he had always been faithful, but I certainly had plenty of doubts about Joan's character, intentions, and purity. Walt had never given me any reason to feel insecure about other women, even when we were miles apart. I stressed again my feelings about the "friendship" he shared with Joan and that her behavior that day showed her true colors.

> *Couples must recognize inappropriate behaviors and change the situation to avoid any possibility of yielding to temptation.*

WALT

Having dinner with another woman several times in her home without my wife showed my naivety and lack of wisdom. As Ikie and I talked and reflected on those past months, I could see how inappropriate my actions had been. I was able to see what Ikie could see and agreed that Joan's behavior showed she had misinterpreted my intentions. Ikie and I had to have open minds. We had to be transparent, sensitive, and flexible in that situation.

Life is inherently challenging, and an emotionally mature person will respond to life's challenges with creativity and sensitivity.

After that conversation, we decided that it was necessary for me to back away from the friendship with Joan. But for weeks after this, she tried to pursue it.

We live in a very permissive society. The norm is to do whatever makes you feel good. In so many cases it appears that young couples enter wedlock with little or no understanding that marriage is sacred and requires maintenance or should I say, "**preventive maintenance**." To provide an understanding of preventive maintenance in a marriage, consider what is meant by preventive maintenance with a car. Preventive maintenance with a car refers to regular, routine maintenance to help keep equipment up and running, preventing any unplanned downtime and expensive costs from unanticipated equipment failure. Therefore, with our cars, we have tune-ups, we have tires rotated, we get regular oil changes and filters. In other words, we do the necessary things to keep the car in good shape.

The same concept is true in a healthy marriage. As I mentioned earlier, boredom is one of numerous reasons for infidelity.

Preventative maintenance is needed
for a healthy, successful marriage.

Partners should participate in activities designed to keep the marriage vibrant and fresh every day in some way. Simple behaviors that strengthen the bond are needed. These behaviors may include, but are not limited to, listening to your partner vent from a frustrating day, planning date nights at home or taking in dinner and a movie, providing pleasant little surprises for each other and doing activities together.

IKIE

It is also necessary to have your own space sometimes. By this, I mean that each partner should have some time away from the other partner. You may wonder why this is necessary.

When a couple is together constantly, it can cause
friction which may result in unnecessary stress.

When partners spend time apart from each other, they tend to enjoy the time they have together even more. Although we enjoy our time together, Walt and I learned years ago that we needed our own space. Over the years, I needed my time to participate in community events and group activities. I have always done some kind of teaching, in church, chapel programs or in the community. I have helped develop mentoring programs and adult education programs throughout our marriage. I love buying and reading books, especially religious materials. He enjoys golfing, exercising, and bowling. He has been the partner who came up with ideas for trips and cruises. Because I do not enjoy technology, he makes all necessary plans. Our different activities necessitated time apart from each other. We intentionally do some activities together such as going to live plays, traveling, and singing in church choirs. When we are together, we enjoy sharing our experiences. These activities and others have strengthened the bond in our marriage.

WALT

Sooner or later in marriages, there will be things seen or realized by a couple that they had not seen or heard during their courtship. Perhaps they were too much in love to see the problem areas before their marriage. According to Erma Bombeck, **"Marriage has no guarantees. If that is what you are looking for, go live with a car battery."** Let's consider just a few examples.

The wife discovers that her new husband is a womanizer. A womanizer typically refers to a man who engages in numerous sexual relationships with women. Suppose he continues those relationships after his marriage. Research shows that men generally engage in womanizing because of low self-esteem, fear of commitment, or conditioning from social media. The wife in this marriage often suffers from emotional distress. She will have feelings of betrayal and distrust which could become a chronic issue for her.

Consider the wife who has such a strong relationship with her family—father or mother that her decisions are swayed by her family's opinions rather than her husband. That can become a real problem! For the husband it feels like the wife is putting her family ahead of him.

Boundaries are absolutely necessary to have healthy relationships.

Couples who do not establish boundaries with others, especially their families, live by an "anything goes" mentality, and your business is my business. Lack of boundaries will allow too much interference from people outside the marriage.

Ikie has no problem with letting me know when something is on her mind. She has learned that I need to know what she expects from me if she wants it done. The practice of telling me her expectations started shortly after I entered the United States Air Force as a young chaplain. As a chaplain, I was often requested to give the invocation for social events on base. Wives were expected to attend. Sometimes, I waited until the last minute to let her know about it. At first, she seemed annoyed that I had not told her, but she hurried and got dressed anyway. One of those times, about an hour before the event was to start, I hurriedly called and said, "We've got a function to attend at 6:00 pm. Hurry up and get dressed, I'll pick you up at 5:45."

She responded, "I'm not going."

"What do you mean, you're not going?" I asked.

"I need you to let me know at least a day before we have to go somewhere. If you can't tell me at least a day before you want me to go, I'm not going. I need time for my hair, my nails, and to choose what I'm going to wear."

Spouses should let their partner know what they expect from them and why.

Ikie had been upset with me for my laxed communication about when events were planned. If she had not shared her expectations, I probably would have continued to forget to tell her.

IKIE

A lasting marriage requires determination and a lot of hard work. Changes, conflicts and discouragements are inevitable when two people live together. Unfortunately, some couples enter marriage with a mindset that should there be problems in the relationship, divorce is always an option. In other words, "if it doesn't work out, I can always get a divorce." Consequently, they are unwilling to do the work to give it a chance to survive. Too often they move on and end the marriage. In my judgment, in those situations, the seeds for divorce are already planted in their minds, even before their wedding day! It will not take much in terms of challenges before the marriage is in serious trouble and without serious counseling and/or serious work by both partners, the marriage will end.

Thankfully, Walt and I worked through the Joan Event and restored our healthy relationship. I love what Paul Tournier says about marriage. He states: "This is what marriage really means: helping one another to reach the full status of being persons, responsible beings who do not run away from life." It took time to communicate our feelings truthfully and explore the "whys" for the "Joan Event," and what it taught us.

We intentionally remembered the "why" of our marriage. We refocused our attention on each other and started doing more activities together. We continued going to church and developed friendships within the church. On Friday evenings after Bible study we went bowling with our new friends.

WALT

The "Joan Event" was a major test for us. Now, after all these years, I know that God was preparing me for the next major event in our lives.

I always have believed that God brought us together and I've never regretted a single day of our marriage! I agree with Jodi Picoult who said, **"I believe in love. I think it just hits you and pulls the rug right out from underneath you and, like a baby, demands your attention every minute of the day."**

REFLECTION AND DISCUSSION QUESTIONS

1. How can couples guard against inappropriate relationships in marriage?

2. Why is faithfulness so vital to a healthy relationship?

3. List two ways faithlessness may negatively impact marriage.

4. Give an example of how couples can practice preventative maintenance in their marriages.

5. Why is it important for spouses to give each other both togetherness and personal space?

Chapter 9

A COMMUNICATION TOOL

"Watch your tongue and keep your mouth shut and you will stay out of trouble."

Proverbs 21:23 (NIV)

"A gentile answer turns away wrath, but a harsh word stirs up anger."

Proverbs 15:1 (NIV)

WALT

One of the most vital components of a healthy marriage is effective communication. During our Joan Event, Ikie and I exhibited **ineffective communication** in two ways. First, she did not effectively let me know that sharing my faith with Joan as faithfully as I did was a **real** problem for her. Second, I did not initially effectively communicate to her that my intentions were innocent.

Many years after our Joan Event, I served as a pastor and a chaplain in the United States Air Force. As a chaplain, I was given the opportunity to receive training in a course known as Parent Effectiveness Training or (PET), developed by Dr. Thomas Gordon. The course was designed to help parents communicate effectively with their children. I believe the communicative skills taught to parents in PET can be successfully adapted for married couples.

This tool provides various techniques of communication in a non-threatening way using the concept of **"active listening and I-messages."** Active listening involves conversation between two people, the person owning the problem and the person perceived as creating the problem. In **active listening**, the person owning the problem clearly states what the problem is but avoids laying blame or accusing the other person. Not only does he or she state clearly what the problem is but also expresses how the problem impacts them. The person who is being impacted by the problem then requests cooperation in solving the problem from the offender in a non-threatening way. For clarification the other person, the offender who is being confronted, restates what he/she heard was the problem. The two individuals may go back and forth in this technique of active listening until a resolution is reached. In active listening, "you-messages" should never be used. The moment the word **YOU** comes out of someone's mouth, it will be perceived as an accusation of the person whether they are guilty or not.

"I-messages" are preferrable because they tell how you feel about the perceived offense and the impact the offense has on you. It also tells how you wish they would correct the offense. I-messages lower the emotional temperature and do not usually put the other person on the defensive. When active listening and I-messages are used effectively the other person sees clearly the problem and its impact and will usually, if reasonable, be willing to cooperate because it makes sense to them.

Let's use a common example. A mother of a teenage daughter confronts her daughter about her room which was dirty, messy, unkempt and like a pigsty! The mother, in a harsh voice converses with a "You message."

"Gina, you're nothing but a slob! Your room is despicable! I'm tired of seeing your room in this condition. I'm giving you an hour to clean it up and keep it clean or the next time I find it like this I'm putting you out of my house and your stuff is going to be on the curb!"

Let's dissect what just happened in this scenario. The mother is angry and perhaps has a right to be angry. However, she has resorted to name-calling, by calling her teenage daughter a slob. She lodges a threat. So now, the emotional temperature between mother and daughter is at a high peak. The relationship between mother and daughter is distant at best. So, what's the fallout of the confrontation from the mother's tirade? It is the hurtful feeling of name-calling. The daughter was called a slob. Name-calling sticks for many years with most people. I have heard the statement, "once something is verbalized, it cannot be retracted." Some people use negative language with the hope of getting positive results. This is called **"reverse psychology."** Reverse psychology does not generally get the positive result expected.

Looking back to that time when Ikie and I were faced with the Joan Event, we certainly could have benefited from this model for healthy communication, using active listening and I-messages. Ikie, in her anger might have said something like, **"Walt, I know that you're trying to be helpful to Joan spiritually, but I have an uneasy feeling that she might have some ulterior motives. If she is successful, that would be devastating to me. So, I would appreciate it if you would curtail your involvement with her for the sake of our marriage."** In this example, Ikie explained the problem she had and the reason. She also described the impact it had on our marriage.

I could have responded by saying **"So, what I hear you saying is you believe Joan is not all she's cracked up to be. She may be trying to drive a wedge between us and break us up. In other words, you don't trust her, right?"** I restated what I understood her to say. She could affirm that I was on target or disagreed with my understanding of what she had said.

If we had used this technique involved with active listening and/or I-messages, we would have felt much less stress. Thankfully, we were able to work through this issue successfully.

REFLECTION AND DISCUSSION QUESTIONS

1. What role does communication play in building trust in marriage?

2. Why are 'I-messages' often more effective than 'you-messages' in difficult conversations?

3. How can active listening help couples resolve conflict?

4. Think of a recent disagreement—how might you have handled it differently using these tools?

Chapter 10

FORGIVENESS

"For if you forgive other people when they sin against you, your heavenly Father will also forgive you. But if you do not forgive others their sins, your father will not forgive your sins."

Matthew 6:14-15 (NIV)

WALT

The Joan Event tested our marriage. I felt that we had the test in preparation for the next major event, which would also test our commitment to each other. I can be very specific about when I accepted Jesus Christ as my personal savior. I cannot be quite as specific about the timing of my "call." However, the way I dealt with Ikie about my call to the ministry resulted in our next major test.

I have talked about our long-distance courtship with Ikie going to school in Missouri and me teaching in Mississippi. I would go to Missouri as often as I could, she came home when she could, and she wrote me often, and I called her as often as I could afford to call So, we were communicating both orally and through writing. At that time, we realized that our relationship was getting more serious and engagement would be the next step in our relationship. During one of our conversations, while Ikie was a student in Missouri, she made a statement that was unusual and certainly unexpected. She casually said, "I do not want my husband to be a doctor or minister." I found her comment puzzling. I was already teaching and these two professions had never crossed my mind. I asked her why she felt that way.

IKIE

When Walt asked me why I did not want my husband's profession to be a minister or doctor, my answer was, "From my experiences and observations, they do not own their lives."

The minister's and his family's expectations put him in a separate category. Let me explain in more detail what I experienced while growing up. On pastoral Sundays, in our small church, the women took turns preparing and serving large meals in their homes after service. Some pastors lived far from the church and did not always bring their families with them. When the family did accompany him, the host family would be delighted. Women would scrub floors, wash curtains, and sweep **dirt** yards. The house had to be perfect when the preacher visited. Children of the host family were to be "seen and not heard."

Community members were often very judgmental of the minister and his family's behavior. The minister was expected to notice the host's clean home and praise them for serving a wonderful meal. If he did not, it would be quietly talked about with other women of the church. His wife was expected to act and dress in a certain way, which seemed to be dictated by an unwritten code. His children were expected to set examples in their behavior as models for the rest of us kids.

Pastors were expected to officiate at weddings and funerals and to visit the sick. Our pastor was often asked to do funerals for unchurched people in the community.

In my mind, there was no consideration of boundaries to give the pastor personal time, vacation time, or time for relaxation for him and his family. To me, a minister's life was dominated by the needs of other people. These are reasons why I did not want my husband to be a minister.

As a nursing student, I have opportunities to interact with residents and interns in the hospital. I see them spending long hours trying to save lives and sometimes losing that battle. I see the emotional turmoil they seemed to experience when they lose a patient. Homer G. Phillips is a city hospital. It is one of the hospitals that cares for some of the sickest and poorest patients. Sometimes members of the medical staff are called right back to the hospital after those long hours if a patient takes a turn for the worse. In other words, to me, doctors cannot be in control of their own lives, patients have to come first.

I know a young man from Kenya who is an intern at the hospital. His name is Sebastian Wahome. There are times when he doesn't have time to eat lunch or dinner. He often works 15 hours or more before he can get some rest. In emergencies, doctors have to drop everything and go.

With ministers, parishioners must come first and with doctors, patients must come first. In both professions, men must devote their lives to needs of other people, not to their families. These are my reasons for not wanting a minister or a doctor for a husband.

WALT

I chuckled at her reasoning because she was so very definite, and specific about her feelings of men in these professions. By now, you are probably wondering what all of this has to do with forgiveness. When we had this discussion, I made a nonchalant statement to her that later became a reason for her to need my forgiveness in our marriage.

"Well, baby, you don't have to worry about me being either one of those. I'm a teacher, and that is what I plan to do. I don't have plans to become a minister or a doctor." At the time, I really meant it. I absolutely had no clue, nor did I have a desire to be a minister or doctor.

I can be very specific about when I gave my life to Jesus Christ and accepted Him as my Savior. I know the place, date, and time when I accepted Christ. However, I am not as specific about "my call." Within months of accepting Christ as my Savior, I felt "the call" to be a minister. This occurred roughly two years after we were married, I accepted God's call to become a minister of the Gospel. I did not share this fact with Ikie.

To be called to the ministry means one accepts and fulfills a God given purpose to serve in Christian ministries. The concept of being called to ministry involves a sense of purpose, a desire to serve others and a recognition of one's spiritual gifts and strengths. A call can be manifested in various ways such as a gradual realization over time, a dramatic encounter with God, or guidance from others. Ultimately, being called into the ministry is about obedience to God's will and a commitment to serving His purpose.

The Great Commission in Matthew 28:18-20 applies to all believers. *Then Jesus came to them and said, "All authority in heaven and on earth has been given to me. Therefore go and make disciples of all nations, baptizing them in the name of the Father and of Son and of the Holy Spirit, and teaching them to obey everything I have commanded you. And surely, I am with you always, to the very end of the age.* Fulfilling our roles as part of the Body of Christ means ministering to others. However, when we hear the phrase "being called," we generally think of being called to serve as a leader of a congregation in some form.

Forgiveness in a marriage refers to a process of letting go of resentment, anger, and hurt towards a spouse after they have caused emotional or psychological pain.

It involves acknowledging the pain caused, choosing to release negative emotions and working towards healing and reconciling a relationship. There are numerous behaviors that a spouse may exhibit that require seeking forgiveness from their spouse. Among these are infidelity, emotional or physical abuse, addiction problems, financial abuse, or unrepentant behavior. Ikie and I had a completely different situation because I was not guilty of any of the behaviors I just mentioned.

But when I accepted my call to the ministry, **I broke a promise I had made to her. To make matters worse, I failed to be transparent with her about it.** Transparency refers to being open, honest, and truthful in communication with your partner.

Partners should share information freely and willingly even if it is uncomfortable or inconvenient.

Ikie did not learn that I had been called to the ministry directly from me. She learned in a very indirect way, by overhearing a conversation between my mother and me.

One of my sisters, who was living in nearby Gary, Indiana, was getting married. My mother had come up to help prepare for the wedding. On the evening of the rehearsal for the wedding, we picked her up from the train station.

Ikie chose to sit in the back seat to let Mama have the more comfortable front seat. We started talking about our jobs and how things were going. Ikie talked about her new job teaching practical nursing students at Provident Hospital and Training School. She was happy to have her new teaching job. She liked it better than being on the nursing staff at Micheal Reese. She rambled on about not having to rotate shifts as she had to do on the nursing staff and how she was learning so much from her teaching experiences with her students. My mother listened to Ikie with great interest, asking questions and adding statements here and there. I was unusually quiet most of the time. My heart was heavy with dread of revealing my call to Ikie and the reality of the effect that could potentially have on our marriage. Ikie had emphatically stated that she did not want a minister for a husband, but I knew **I had no choice** about becoming one.

I received confirmation of my call from several sources. First, my interest in teaching had severely faded. I was much more interested in aspects of the Gospel.

Secondly, my father-in-law, Mr. Haynes, had unexpectantly called. Usually, when we got calls from her parents, Mother Lillie would make the call. Mr. Haynes had never called himself before.

We chatted briefly, and then he made a comment that jarred me. His words to me were, **"Walter, I may not live to see it, but you are going to preach one day."** I remember looking at the phone, trying to determine if I had heard him correctly. As he continued to talk, I learned that he had been experiencing "these feelings" about me preaching. He felt that I was supposed to preach, and he wanted me to know.

Interestingly, Mr. Haynes had never talked to me about preaching before but, apparently, he had been having these feelings for several weeks.

Thirdly, my oldest sister's husband had also called to describe a dream my sister had. In the dream, our father was preaching on our farm from the back of a wagon. Even though it was our dad, in her dream, he was a much younger person. From the description of my sister's dream, my brother-in-law, a minister, surmised that it was not our dad preaching, but *me* instead. Fourthly, I was consumed with a great desire to share God's Word and minister to others.

I knew it was time to make the fact of my call known. What better time to do so while sitting next to Mama, someone who has been a source of emotional support all my life.

Just before we reached the church, I whispered to Mama, "I think I have been called to the ministry."

I've been praying for a sign and God has given them to me.

I'm not sure how Mama responded. But Ikie, who hears well, even to this day, sat up and leaned toward the front and loudly said, **"You've been what?"**

From the tone and pitch of her voice, I knew she was shocked, maybe even angry. Fortunately, we had gotten to the church and had to get out of the car. We did not have an opportunity to continue the discussion at that time. I silently prayed as we went into the church,

"Lord, you have to help me deal with this situation. It will not be easy."

Needless to say, I was distracted by the activities of the wedding rehearsal all evening. My mind was on the conversation Ikie and I had to have later when we went home.

As the evening passed, I remembered some passages of scripture that gave me a sense of peace and had a consoling effect on my psyche.

We serve a God who can speak and cause stars to appear in the sky. God can heal people with leprosy. God can calm seas and summon legions of angels. He can bring water from a rock and part the sea. He can rain food from heaven and make a virgin conceive. He can bring dead men back to life and put coins in the mouth of fish. He can cast demons into the bodies of swine. Surely, He will help me deal with Ikie and reconcile our healthy relationship.

Forgiveness is a critical component of successful marriages. Forgiveness helps couples move past conflicts, rebuild trust and strengthen their emotional connection.

Although one cannot go back in time and change what has been done, you can and should ask the spouse for forgiveness. When you ask a spouse for forgiveness you don't pretend that nothing has happened. In my case, I had to follow God's call, even though it meant that I had to go against what I had promised my wife. My approach was to ask her not to hold this against me. Obedience to my call was the best option for me. My main concern was that I had not told her about it. I had not lied to her, but I had not been open and honest about it. I had to ask for forgiveness because I had broken a promise I had made before we were married.

Forgiveness benefits both partners in the relationship because it gives them a chance to let go of the grudge they may be carrying and start the process of healing and restoration.

Obviously, Ikie forgave me, because we have had a wonderful, long marriage in which Ikie was supportive in all my pastoral duties. I was a civilian pastor for ten years and served as a chaplain in the United States Air Force for 27 years.

In fact, Ikie has taken many roles of leadership right by my side. I must admit that our issues requiring forgiveness were not as severe as many other couples who have a need for a fresh start. However, there are some people who refuse to forgive. There are some serious adverse effects from not being a forgiving partner. Unforgiveness can impact any marriage.

WALT & IKIE

When forgiveness is withheld, unresolved hurt accumulates and creates bitterness in the offended partner.

This resentment can fester over time and lead to frustration, negative thoughts, and severely negative behaviors. The offended partner may not physically harm the offender but refuses to try to make amends and tries to make their partner's life a living hell. Naturally, this results in a very toxic relationship.

We personally know of a couple whose marriage was miserable because the husband had an affair before his marriage. That affair produced two children who were born before his marriage. The husband denied the affair and the children to his fiancée before the marriage. The wife found out years after their marriage that he had lied. The husband repented. He was very sorry for the lies and deceit. He recognized the pain, hurt and disappointment he had caused his wife, but he loved her and did not want to lose her. So, he lied over and over about it all. By the time he admitted the truth to his wife, the couple had children. The wife did not want her children to miss out on having their father in their lives. She stayed in the marriage. But due to the lack of forgiveness, she was miserable, she made the husband miserable and the children, sensing the constant tension, were also miserable.

We will not suggest whether or not the couple should have stayed in the marriage. People should make the choices they feel are best for them. But some choices have "unfixable consequences." The question must be asked, "Would it have been better for the wife in this situation to stay in the marriage without forgiveness or leave and share the parenting of their children separately?" We understand that the wife decided to stay married, for the sake of the children, but at what cost?

Forgiveness can be one of the most challenging parts of maintaining a healthy relationship.

In the situation we just described, trust was broken, and emotional scars were created in the husband, the wife and most likely in the children.

Forgiveness is vital in relationships. Without forgiveness, couples tend to emotionally withdraw from each other. Because of unresolved conflicts invisible walls are created in the marriage and it becomes difficult, if not impossible, to openly share how each partner really feels. There will be a tendency to mask true feelings. Over time, the partners lose closeness and affection for each other. Due to these unresolved conflicts some couples, who have had long marriages, simply "live together." They don't sleep in the same room or even eat their meals together. In some cases people are seen by others as grumpy people because of the severe negativity they have in their lives. Generally, these people are difficult to be around. They are incapable of being joyful or pleasant in any setting. Emotional detachment makes for an unhealthy psyche. They are complainers, finding fault not only with their spouse but also with others who cross their paths.

"It's better to live alone in the desert than with a quarrel-some, complaining wife."

Proverbs 21:19 (NIV)

When issues go unforgiven, they often come up again in future arguments.

The same conflict, subject, or offense, will be repeated over and over in future arguments. We have heard partners say things like "she just keeps bringing the same thing up" or "if we have moved past that why do you continue to mention it?" There is a vicious cycle of negativity between the partners. Neither of them will feel heard or validated. This often results in even more escalated conflicts. Small disagreements can then turn into bigger problems for the couple.

WALT

Without forgiveness a couple will find that rebuilding trust is much harder, if not impossible.

When partners are suspicious or doubtful of each other, the stability of the relationship weakens. They then become vulnerable to hearsay and gossip about the spouse. There is one couple I recall in a counseling session who were dealing with this issue of lacking trust because of unforgiveness. The wife had been unfaithful on one occasion in their marriage. The husband stated that he had forgiven her but remained suspicious of everything she did. Even when she shopped for groceries, he was suspicious that she was being unfaithful. His lack of forgiveness created uncertainty, making them both feel insecure about the future of their marriage. He never understood that his lack of genuine forgiveness was necessary in order to begin the process of rebuilding trust.

Forgiveness allows relationships
to heal and progress.

IKIE

If couples do not forgive, the relationship becomes stagnant and cannot grow. All of us, including married people, should learn from our mistakes. As I mentioned in one of the earlier chapters, none of us are perfect. Anne Lamott, an American novelist, has a favorite quote: **"Refusing to forgive someone else is like drinking rat poison and expecting the rat to die."**

WALT

I recall another example in which unforgiveness led to a complete state of family dysfunction. This couple had been married for approximately ten years and had at least two children. The husband was domineering and egotistical. He worked away from home and was not affectionate. The wife sought satisfaction for her sexual needs through an affair with another man for several years. She repeatedly lied to her husband about the affair, but he knew she was lying. The wife discovered that some community members were aware of what she was doing. This forced her to eventually own up to the affair. She begged her husband for forgiveness. She understood that she was wrong, but she felt he owned some responsibility for their broken marriage as well. He never felt that he did.

By the time the wife admitted that the rumors were true, the husband had grown stony, cold, and bitter. He stayed in the marriage. It's almost as though he stayed in the marriage to punish his wife. He taught the children to despise their mother. Now that woman, an adulterer, is very ill, bed-bound. She cannot perform any of her daily needs. She is totally dependent on one child who helps her some. Besides this, the husband refuses to allow any of her family members to help.

What a travesty!

It is necessary to seek some form of counseling to cross a hurdle this dire.

> ***If one in the union cannot find
> a way to forgive, one of the two probably
> should dissolve the marriage.***

IKIE

Mistakes are made in marriages as they often are in life. Each time a couple realizes their mistakes, take ownership of them, and forgive, they can find a way to grow. It is through transparency, sensitivity and effective communication that understanding and resolution occurs. Unless a couple reaches the place of forgiveness, the marriage is usually in serious trouble. However, if they can achieve forgiveness, the relationship is strengthened, and they can grow stronger together.

Without forgiveness partners will feel trapped in the cycle of blame and defense. This pattern of conflict prevents their relationship from growing and becoming stable.

REFLECTION AND DISCUSSION QUESTIONS

1. Why is forgiveness so vital in marriage?

2. What happens to a relationship when unforgiveness is allowed to linger?

3. How can couples rebuild trust after it has been broken?

4. What role does transparency play in maintaining a healthy marriage?

5. Why is it important to learn to forgive not just for your spouse's sake, but for your own emotional and spiritual health?

Chapter 11

PARENTING

"Start children off on the way they should go, and even when they are old they will not turn from it."

Proverbs 22:6 (NIV)

Our children, Angie and Tony

IKIE

I have always referred to our daughter, Angela (Angie), as our "social butterfly" or our "flower child." Moving from place to place, which was necessary due to the nature of Walt's work, only bothered Angie during the move. Naturally, she hated leaving her established friendships and the familiarity of the area. Once we were relocated and she got involved with a group of kids or if she met one new little girl, she was able to successfully adapt to the new location. Shortly after our moves, she would come home and tell us about her new friend or new friends. Not only did she make friends easily she kept friends for long periods, even after we relocated to another place.

Walter Anthony (Tony), our son, was just the opposite. Similar to Walt in many ways, he did not make friends easily. In fact, I had to strongly encourage him to get involved in kid activities on the base. I referred to him as our "what if" child. Tony would project his fears into statements like, "what if they don't like me?" or "what if I don't make the team?" He was not a social butterfly in that once he made a friend, that was his best friend, he didn't worry about making others. In contrast to Angie who wanted to be going and doing, Where Angie wanted to be going and doing, Tony was content to stay home and play with his toys or with the Nintendo gaming system.

Before Walt entered the U.S. Air Force, we had an opportunity to visit a U.S. Air Force chaplain and his wife who had been in the service for many years. The chaplain's wife made two suggestions to me that served to be invaluable in helping our children adjust to moves during Walt's military career. First, get your home set up as soon as possible. In doing this try to arrange the household goods as close as possible to how they were at your last home. This will naturally help the children feel like they are at "home." Second, get the children involved in activities that include other children. Interacting with children their age, who are experiencing similar lives, seemed to help our children to understand that they were not "different." Because of the camaraderie established with other children on the bases, our children were able to make the necessary adjustments in difficult situations.

Parents should make appropriate efforts to help their children adjust to new environments.

Parents should remember that each child is different. Even identical twins are strikingly different in some ways. Some of the areas of differences include mental health, cognitive abilities, personalities, emotions, sexuality, friendships. Because of differences, we had to parent each of our children in different ways often incorporating a combination of parenting styles.

Ikie and kids on the beach

One Sunday, after church when we were driving home, I thought about this scripture that was quoted at the beginning of this chapter and how much it applied to us. My immediate thoughts went to our parents, and their parenting styles. Their styles influenced the parenting styles we used with our children.

The dictionary defines parenting as, "the act of bringing up a child as a parent."

The old people—often referred to when I was a child—called parenting, "raising a child." Other people refer to parenting as "taking care of someone as a parent. Experts have categorized and defined various parenting styles.

Authoritative: Supposedly, this style is considered the ideal style because it includes both warmth and flexibility, while maintaining parental authority in the home. These parents set boundaries for the children, so the children know what is expected of them. The parents establish rules and explain the consequences of violating or breaking the rules. In this style parents listen to the child's opinion but remain the primary decision maker.

Permissive: These parents pride themselves on being the child's best friend. They are warm and nurturing and have "open" communication. Discipline is used, sparingly. They allow the child to make their own choices and bail them out of the consequences of poor or bad choices. These children have the freedom to make decisions like what to eat, when to go to bed and whether to do their homework. They may be impulsive, demanding and lack the ability to regulate themselves or have self-control. Rather than use any parental control of the child, permissive parents try to control the child's environment.

Authoritarian: These are strict parents with strict rules. These parents have high standards and control the child's behavior with harsh punishment. The child is expected to perform at high levels without exceptions. These parents are never flexible, and children may not be aware that a rule is in place until the child is punished for breaking the rule. Children in these homes could become aggressively rebellious, lack social skills, may have difficulty making sound decisions on their own and possibly lousy spouses.

Neglectful: These are the parents who offer minimal nurturing and have few expectations or limitations of their children. They simply fulfill the child's basic physical needs, providing little if any emotional attention to the child. This parenting style may not be the choice the parent wants to have but is forced because the parent must work late and long shifts, they may have unmet emotional and psychological needs themselves, or there may be troublesome other issues in the home that cause the parent to neglect the child.

WALT

Ikie and I were raised by parents who had combinations of authoritarian and authoritative styles of parenting. In other words, they were caring, provided for our physical needs but set boundaries that we knew and understood we were not to cross.

My father was a stern disciplinarian. In my book, *Inmates in Charge*, I described one of the worst whippings I ever got from my dad because I broke one of his rules. He was the principal of our elementary school and one of his rules, of which I was aware, was "no smoking by any student." One day, because I was influenced by peer pressure, he found me smoking. To demonstrate how serious this was, he made an example of me that day by whipping me in front of my peers who had snitched on me to him.

One Sunday after church the Scripture which begins this chapter came to me and I thought about smoking and that whipping. I crossed an established boundary and got a whipping for it that I remember to this day! I have friends who are nearly chain smokers.

But I do not smoke. There was a brief time, in college, that I did after I became an adult. I did not enjoy it. I think I smoked just to be defiant and prove that I was grown and could do whatever I wanted with my own life. Sometimes children become defiant and rebellious because of severe parental boundaries. Fortunately for me, my smoking did not last, I could move on from "do not smoke" but I did not move too far from some aspects of my dad's authoritative style of parenting.

Ikie and I practiced a combination of parenting styles with our children. We learned early that our children were smarter than we were and would push established, if we allowed them to, or they would not take the boundaries seriously. I was more of a disciplinarian or authority figure in parenting our children. Although Ikie was sometime authoritative, most often she was more permissive. She did not set rigid boundaries, and our children knew that. Our children could wear her down by continually begging to get what they wanted.

**Parents should discuss and set parameters
with children and stay firm in keeping them.**

IKIE

Mama was warm and nurturing, but firm. She exhibited a "matter of fact" way of dealing with us. She frequently reminded us of her expectations or asked if we had finished a chore. She seldom raised her voice above conversational tones. She was very disciplined and prompt with time and responsibilities. On Saturday evenings, she would comb our hair for church the next day and tie it up. She pressed our dresses and cleaned our shoes if necessary. We were usually the first family at church for Sunday school. She was a Sunday School teacher.

Daddy was playful and jovial. When I was a tiny girl, he would chase us through the house and pick us up. We screamed with delight when daddy played with us. He always told us how much he loved us and made us feel that we could do anything. His goal for us was for us to be independent. He encouraged us to study hard and excel.

Despite his playfulness, he could be very firm. If we were acting up in church, Daddy would simply look at the one misbehaving in church and shake his head or wave his finger to let us know, without speaking, "that's enough; stop what you are doing or you will be in trouble." When we visited other people's homes our parents did not have to say, "sit down" or "don't touch." We knew our boundaries in that setting and we were obedient.

Boundaries provide a sense of safety, create consistency, teach responsibility, help develop self-control, and improve the children's ability to effectively communicate.

WALT

Soon after our children were old enough to talk and have their own personalities, we learned that we had to have a united front with them. Ikie and I learned to confer frequently about what the children asked, or they would play one of us against the other to get what they wanted. For example, the children would come to me for something they wanted. I would say, "No" or "I'll think about it." They would then go to Ikie and say, "Daddy said I could." Thinking they were telling her the truth, she would also approve, she would find out later that I actually had said no or I'll think about it. We call that "manipulating the possibilities" to get what they wanted.

Therefore, we started conferring directly with each other to prevent any confusion.

Both parents should be united in making decisions regarding their children.

IKIE

With a united front, neither parent ought to be angry about being excluded from the decision-making process. It avoids repressed feelings caused by a parent's inability or unwillingness to be confrontative or verbally expressive when one is not involved in the decision-making process. It provides a positive role model for the child to establish foundations for parenting in their future. As with individuals and marriages, parenting is never perfect individuals are different, marriages are different and parenting is different. Parents must find a parenting style or process that works best for their family. Many parents use a combination of parenting styles. We feel that consistency is important so children are never confused about expectations.

REFLECTION AND DISCUSSION QUESTIONS

1. How has your own upbringing influenced your own parenting style?

2. Why is it important for parents to present a 'united front' when raising children?

3. How can setting boundaries help children feel safe and develop responsibility?

Chapter 12

AGING GRACIOUSLY AND GRACEFULLY

"The glory of young men is their strength, gray hair the splendor of the old."

Proverb 20:29 (NIV)

WALT

When Ikie and I were children, in our young minds, people of advanced age seemed to be ancient. Many also seemed angry most of the time. I used to wonder why Uncle John always had a sour expression on his face and mumbled in his throat whenever he spoke. I can also remember when I would feel a sense of pity and helplessness when I saw old men struggle to stand from sitting. Once they managed to stand up, they would stand in that spot for several minutes. It was as though they stood motionless for a while to let their body parts settle before moving. Then when they did begin to move, they walked with short unsteady steps. If they did not have a "walking stick" or cane they would hold on to walls or any solid structure to help them make their steps.

At such a tender age, I did not understand the challenges that Golden-agers face or how those challenges could impact their dispositions. If they were asked how they felt, the usual answers included: "I'm getting by," "I'm just making it," "one day at a time," "I'm just here, and that's all," etc. These responses were given with stern faces and frowns. **"Now that we've gotten older, everything is finally starting to click for us—our knees, our backs, our necks…"** As a very young child I was sometimes fearful of elderly people because of their behaviors but even at a young age I decided that I would not ever be like those "old" people.

Now that Ikie and I are seniors, we realize that aging is not an easy process. Seniors may be gruff or grumpy and have sour dispositions for a combination of emotional, psychological, and physical factors. These include the loss of health, having lost their independence, and social connections, hormonal changes, economic concerns, and chronic pain. With the many challenges that come with aging, it is natural for seniors to feel down and sometimes discouraged.

Many seniors have little, if any, savings, and inadequate health insurance. The expenses associated with housing maintenance, food, and health needs seem to increase as we age. If people don't have proper insurance or help from their children or other family members, they often face uncertain days. Ikie sacrificed a great deal when I was on active duty in the military. She was unable to have a career of her own due to us moving every 3-4 years. She was a registered nurse with a master's degree in human development counseling. She found work at all of my assignments except the last two in which she elected not to work. I realized, early in my career, that she would not have retainability at any job long enough to have a retirement income later in her life. I had the foresight to start an annuity/IRA for her during my first assignment to offset her not being able to have her own career. Now that we are seniors, she has found economic comfort from my foresightedness many years ago.

Despite the life challenges we face as we age, most people's goal is to live long enough to realize the fruits of old age. But we want to do it graciously and gracefully, with as little pain and discomfort as possible. Aging is a journey that is inevitable. The way we approach this process can impact the quality of life for all of us, including our partner and other people, including young children, in our social circle.

Growing old gracefully and graciously are approaches to aging which show our mindset and dictate our actions and attitudes.

There are often times when Ikie is asked how she is feeling, she will say, "I'm doing pretty good." What she means by that is that she is not doing great but she could do better. She has learned to accept the wrinkles in her face and neck, acknowledge that arthritis is chronic and knows that she will have gray hair unless she dyes it. I am just the opposite, I will loudly say that I'm doing great, especially when I consider alternatives. Periodically, I visit nursing homes or patients in the hospital, then remind myself that I'm highly blessed when I put life into perspective. With reluctance, I have learned to accept the fact that I cannot lift weights as heavy as I used to and I cannot hit the golf ball as far as I use to, but that's ok!

Avoidance of depression is achieved by acceptance of the changes that come with aging.

IKIE

Despite of the physical, intellectual, and emotional impacts we experience with aging, individuals must be proactive in maintaining as much pleasure in life as possible as they age. Dr. John Dunlop, a gerontologist, author of *Finishing Well to the Glory of God*, has suggested two rules for staying mentally healthy as we age. "First, wake up every morning knowing what you are going to do that day. Second, go to bed every night knowing that you have helped someone."

The benefit of these rules for seniors is developing a richer appreciation for how the Lord can use us every new morning.

> *"Is not wisdom found among the aged? Does not long life bring understanding?"*
>
> Job 12:12 (NIV)

As we enter new chapters in our lives, some of us may feel that we are too busy, too weak, or too old to serve God. But older people have wisdom. If we cannot do anything else we can share that wisdom with others, our children, and our grandchildren. The Christian life is about serving God throughout our entire lives. Serving Him includes the use of wisdom for others.

WALT

Satan loves to use the giants of discouragement and despair typically experienced by aging people. These negative feelings are designed to cause seniors to doubt their faith. If we allow despair and discouragement to control our spirit, our lives will be dominated by them and we will experience despair and depression. We must remember that negative feelings come when we try to evaluate the current circumstances in our life without recognizing that God has ordained the order of our lives. We must accept the order of the life that God has ordained. In other words, when we see the challenges and limitations that we face today and compare them to what our lives *use* to be, we have the tendency to get discouraged. It is natural to remember what was. But it is not natural to continually dwell on the differences between the now and what is the past. Scripture has provided instructions that should help us in our efforts to avoid despair or discouragement. It says,

> *"Be strong and courageous. Do not be afraid; do not be discouraged, for the Lord your God will be with you wherever you go."*

Joshua 1:9 (NIV)

If possible, seniors should put themselves in environments with others for conversation, information, laughter and caring. I have joined a veteran's bowling league, and I still play golf though not as often as I did five years ago. Ikie sews with a group as a ministry in our church and both of us sing in our church choir.

Seniors should seize opportunities for interactions with others to maintain balanced mental health.

Older people should make every effort to be more positive in their actions and thoughts. Instead of dwelling on missed opportunities in life, our limitations and health concerns, we should focus on the things we can do and the positive impact we may have on others. For example, during and after my devotional time, which I do each morning after getting my coffee, frequently a name of someone runs across my mind. When that happens, I make it practice to pick up the phone and call that person. Most often that person is either sick or has been and is happy to hear from me and will often say, "I am so glad to hear from you." That has had a positive impact on the individual and on me. Ikie has a similar devotional routine each morning in addition to a weekly women's Bible study. These activities have enhanced our spiritual life and our marriage.

As we have matured in age, we have also made changes in our eating habits. These new habits have improved our physical health. We have adopted an eating plan using most of the foods we grew up eating. Since the foods are familiar to us, we feel we are apt to continue using our food plan for the rest of our lives. We chose to learn to eat differently for health reasons. I have diabetes which is inherited and Ikie has pulmonary hypertension accompanied by congestive heart failure. We were both severely overweight. Since we have adopted our plan, my endocrinologist reduced some of my diabetic medications, Ikie's weight is significantly less, our mobility has improved, and our energy level has increased.

Individuals should seek new ways of living which may improve their quality of life.

I began exercising regularly while on active duty in the Air Force, in fact it was required of each person. After retirement 23 years ago, I never stopped going to the gym. I have continued that practice to this day at the ripe old age of 85. Ikie has walked for many years and now goes to the gym. I generally go to the gym for one and a half hours, 3 times a week. I believe that I am more physically fit today than I was at the age of 25. Ikie goes to the gym less and stays for a shorter period. But her physical abilities are better than many 84-year-old women.

Exercising the body on a regular basis is paramount to good physical and mental health.

Becoming more forgetful is expected in elderly people. To help us stay on track, we write notes on stickies as reminders. As soon as calendars for the new year are available, we get one. If we have been given annual medical appointments a year in advance, we put them on the calendar. We try to look at the following week's appointments every Sunday. I remind Ikie of hers and she often reminds me of mine.

We look for opportunities and new experiences that expand our minds and improve our intellectual abilities. Included among these are going to movies, attending live drama presentations, joining groups, and participating in word and card games. We have done extensive traveling and still enjoy traveling both in and out of the country. As the years pass, our activities on cruises have lessened. But we still enjoy meeting new people and experiencing any new thing that we can.

We share as many meals as possible together. Conversation and companionship are vital to us. We empathize with people who have lost their spouse and thank God daily for the blessing of each other. In our quiet moments together, we often silently enjoy seeing the birds feeding at the feeder, or listening to the raindrops on a rainy day, or feeling the fall breeze. We are grateful God brought us together when we were so young at that October dance many years ago.

REFLECTION AND DISCUSSION QUESTIONS

1. What does aging graciously and gracefully mean to you?

2. What practical steps can couples take to maintain health and joy in their later years?

3. How can seniors avoid discouragement and find renewed purpose in life?

4. Why is community and social connection important as people grow older?

5. What role does gratitude and perspective play in aging well?

More Memories that Made us

Snapshots of a Love That Endures

Shaw Temple AME Zion Church
where Walt was Senior Pastor

Ikie in Chicago, 1965

Ikie and Angela in 1973

Walt's promotion to colonel. Ikie and Tony pinning on his rank.

Walt making remarks with his departure from Keesler AFB

Walt & Ikie in South Korea

Ikie & Tony at the DMZ in South Korea

Epilogue

As we bring this book to a close, we want to leave you with one final reflection. Throughout these chapters, we have shared lessons from our marriage that we pray will strengthen and inspire couples of every generation. We began with role modeling from our parents and have walked you through the values, struggles, and choices that have carried us through more than 60 years together.

But marriage is not only about starting well; it is also about finishing well. As younger couples build their homes, we want them also to picture the journey ahead. One day, by God's grace, you too will reach the later seasons of life. The choices you make now will determine how you experience those years.

This Epilogue is our personal testimony of what it means to **grow older side by side**, facing the realities of aging while still holding on to joy, faith, and love. While younger couples may not yet feel the weight of these experiences, they can benefit from seeing the road that lies ahead. For couples who share our season of life, we pray these words remind you that aging is not a loss, but an opportunity to show grace, courage, and gratitude together.

So, as you step into the future, whether in the early years of marriage or the golden years, our encouragement remains the same: lean on God, love one another, and embrace each day with hope. We are living proof that marriage can last- not because we are perfect, but because we chose to keep trying, keep forgiving, and keep God first.

Closing Blessing

May the Lord bless your marriage with steadfast love, unshakable faith, and a joy that grows deeper with each passing year. May your home be filled with peace, your hearts with forgiveness, and your journey with purpose.

As you walk hand in hand, may you always remember that God is the third strand that holds you together, and with Him, your love can endure all things. May your covenant be a testimony of grace for generations to come. **AMEN**

Acknowledgments

We give sincere thanks to our endorsers: Dr. Tim Walker, Dr. Robert L. Jemerson, Rev. Reginald Buckley, Rev. John Paul Ruth, MSgt.(Ret.) Marshall Rainge, Dr. Merchuria Chase Williams, Mrs. Paige Stowe, Lt. Col. (Ret.) M.K. Barnes, Dr. John McCoy, CW5 Gordon Smith(Ret.), and Mrs. Dorothy W. Williams, who contributed the Foreword.

We also thank our publisher, Ms. Willa Robinson, and her team, who provided guidance and encouragement. She graciously endorsed this project.

Finally, thanks to our family and friends for their prayers and encouragement.

About the Authors

Chaplain Colonel (Retired) **Walter E. Beamon** served 27 distinguished years as a U.S. Air Force Chaplain, with assignments that spanned the globe. A trailblazer in his field, he became only the **ninth African American Chaplain (USAF-active duty)** to achieve the rank of Colonel—a milestone reached by just 30 African American chaplains in the seventy-eight-year history of the Air Force. No African American chaplain (USAF-active duty) has been promoted beyond the rank of Colonel.

Throughout his career, Chaplain Colonel Beamon broke numerous barriers of leadership and service:

- First African American Chaplain to serve as Wing Chaplain at Keesler AFB (1993–1997)

- First African American Chaplain to serve as Command Chaplain, HQ USSCOM (1997–1999)

- First African American Chaplain to serve as Command Chaplain, HQ AFSOC (1999–2002)

- First African American minister to serve as Associate Pastor and later Pastor Emeritus at First United Methodist Church in Crestview, Florida

After retiring from the Air Force in 2002, he continued his ministry at First United Methodist Church in Crestview, Florida, a predominantly White, conservative congregation, where he served from 2002 to 2005 and was later honored as **Pastor Emeritus** in 2014.

He is the **author of the award-winning memoir,** *Inmates in Charge: Top-Level Leadership—Lacking Vision, Corrupt, & Couldn't Be Trusted*, which exposes the systemic barriers faced by African American chaplains and calls for integrity and inclusion in leadership.

With this new work, *A Marriage That Endures Forever: Our Journey, Your Path to a Healthy Marriage,* Chaplain Colonel Beamon and his wife, **Ikie**, share the wisdom, faith, and commitment that have sustained their own enduring marriage.

He holds a BS degree from Tougaloo College, Jackson, Mississippi; a Master of Divinity (M. Div.); from Virginia Union School of Theology, Richmond, Virginia; and a Master of Theology (M.Th.) from Union Theological Seminary, Richmond, Virginia.

A devoted husband, father, grandfather, and great-grandfather, Chaplain Colonel Beamon resides in **Madison, Mississippi**, where his life continues to reflect his steadfast dedication to **faith, family, and service**.

Ikie H. Beamon is a native of Carson, Mississippi, in Jefferson Davis County. After graduating from high school, she attended Tougaloo College in Jackson, Mississippi, earning a Bachelor of Science degree in 1964. She also graduated from the Homer G. Phillips Hospital School of Nursing in St. Louis, Missouri, earning her Diploma in Registered Nursing.

In 1981, while living in England, Ikie earned a Master of Education in Human Development Counseling from George Peabody College for Teachers through Vanderbilt University's Overseas Program. Her graduation ceremonies were held at the historic Oxford University in England.

Throughout her career, Ikie's professional experiences have been diverse and far-reaching as she accompanied her husband, Chaplain Colonel (Ret.) Walter E. Beamon, during his 27-year U.S. Air Force career. Her work has included roles as a hospital staff nurse, home health nurse, and nursing instructor for licensed practical nursing students, associate degree candidates, and college students. She has also taught health education at the high school and elementary levels.

Ikie played a key role in developing the Utilization Review Program for Hughes Spalding of Grady Hospital in Atlanta, Georgia, and a Quality Assurance Program for Gulf Coast Community Hospital in Mississippi.

A lifelong learner and creative spirit, Ikie enjoys writing children's stories and adult dramas, as well as reading inspirational literature. She resides in Madison, Mississippi, with her husband, Walt. *A Marriage That Endures Forever: Our Journey, Your Path to a Healthy Marriage* is her first published book.

www.ingramcontent.com/pod-product-compliance
Lightning Source LLC
Chambersburg PA
CBHW051521120626
46551CB00012B/1022